This book is to be returned on or before
the last date stamped below.

BROMLEY COLLEGE

Library

of Further & Higher Education

WITHDRAWN

Latest titles in the McGraw-Hill Training Series

EVALUATING TRAINING EFFECTIVENESS 2nd edition
Benchmarking your Training Activity Against Best Practice
Peter Bramley   ISBN 0-07-709028-4
DEVELOPING A LEARNING CULTURE
Empowering People to Deliver Quality, Innovation and Long-term Success
Sue Jones   ISBN 0-07-707983-3
THE CREATIVE TRAINER
Holistic Facilitation Skills for Accelerated Learning
Michael Lawlor and Peter Handley   ISBN 0-07-709030-6
DEVELOPING EFFECTIVE TRAINING SKILLS 2nd edition
A Practical Guide to Designing and Delivering Group Training
Tony Pont   ISBN 0-07-709143-4
CROSS-CULTURAL TEAM BUILDING
Guidelines for More Effective Communication and Negotiation
Mel Berger   ISBN 0-07-707919-1
LEARNING TO CHANGE
A Resource for Trainers, Managers and Learners Based on Self-Organized Learning
Sheila Harri-Augstein and Ian M. Webb   ISBN 0-07-707896-9
ASSESSMENT AND DEVELOPMENT IN EUROPE
Adding Value to Individuals and Organizations
Edited by Mac Bolton   ISBN 0-07-707928-0
PRACTICAL INSTRUCTIONAL DESIGN FOR OPEN LEARNING
MATERIALS
A Modular Course Covering Open Learning, Computer-based Training and
Multimedia
Nigel Harrison   ISBN 0-07-709055-1
DELIVERING IN-HOUSE OUTPLACEMENT
A Practical Guide for Trainers, Managers and Personnel Specialists
Alan Jones   ISBN 0-07-707895-0
FACILITATION
Providing Opportunities For Learning
Trevor Bentley   ISBN 0-07-707684-2
DEVELOPMENT CENTRES
Realizing the Potential of Your Employees Through Assessment and Development
Geoff Lee and David Beard   ISBN 0-07-707785-7
DEVELOPING DIRECTORS
Building an Effective Boardroom Team
Colin Coulson-Thomas   ISBN 0-07-707590-0
MANAGING THE TRAINING PROCESS
Putting the Basics into Practice
Mike Wills   ISBN 0-07-707806-3
HOW TO SUCCEED IN EMPLOYEE DEVELOPMENT 2nd edition
Moving from vision to results
Ed Moorby   ISBN 0-07-709151-5

Details of these and other titles in the series are available from:

The Product Manager, Professional Books, McGraw-Hill Publishing Company,
Shoppenhangers Road, Maidenhead, Berkshire SL6 2QL, United Kingdom
Tel: 01628 23432 Fax: 01628 770224

Workplace Counselling

Developing the skills in managers

Di Kamp

The McGraw-Hill Companies

London · New York · St Louis · San Francisco · Auckland
Bogotá · Caracas · Lisbon · Madrid · Mexico · Milan
Montreal · New Delhi · Panama · Paris · San Juan · São Paulo
Singapore · Sydney · Tokyo · Toronto

Published by
McGRAW-HILL Publishing Company
Shoppenhangers Road, Maidenhead, Berkshire SL6 2QL, England
Telephone: 01628 23432
Fax: 01628 770224

British Library Cataloguing in Publication Data
Kamp, Di
  Workplace counselling: developing the skills in managers.
  – (McGraw-Hill training series)
  1. Employees – Counselling of 2. Counselling 3. Interpersonal
  relations 4. Personnel Management
  I. Title
  658.3'85

  ISBN 0-07-709152-3

Library of Congress Cataloging-in-publication Data
Kamp, Di
  Workplace counselling: developing the skills in managers / Di
Kamp.
     p.   cm. – (The McGraw-Hill training series)
  Includes bibliographical references and index.
  ISBN 0-07-709152-3 (alk. paper)
  1. Employees—Counselling of. 2. Executives—Training of.
I. Title   II. Series.
HF5549.5.C8K35   1996
658.4'071244–dc20

                                                           96-7996
                                                              CIP

McGraw-Hill
A Division of The **McGraw·Hill** Companies

12345 CUP 99876

Typeset by BookEns Limited, Royston, Herts
and printed and bound in Great Britain at the University Press, Cambridge

Printed on permanent paper in compliance with ISO Standard 9706

Contents

Series preface

Training and development are now firmly centre stage in most, if not all, organizations. Nothing unusual in that—for some organizations. They have always seen training and development as part of the heart of their businesses—but more and more must see it that same way.

The demographic trends through the 1990s will inject into the market-place severe competition for good people who will need good training. Young people without conventional qualifications, skilled workers in redundant crafts, people out of work, women wishing to return to work—all will require excellent training to fit them to meet the job demands of the 1990s and beyond.

But excellent training does not spring from what we have done well in the past. T&D specialists are in a new ball game. 'Maintenance' training—training to keep up skill levels to do what we have always done—will be less in demand. Rather, organization, work and market change training are now much more important and will remain so for some time. Changing organizations and people is no easy task, requiring special skills and expertise which, sadly, many T&D specialists do not possess.

To work as a 'change' specialist requires us to get to centre stage—to the heart of the company's business. This means we have to ask about future goals and strategies, and even be involved in their development, at least as far as T&D policies are concerned.

This demands excellent communication skills, political expertise, negotiating ability, diagnostic skills—indeed, all the skills a good internal consultant requires.

The implications for T&D specialists are considerable. It is not enough merely to be skilled in the basics of training, we must also begin to act like business people and to think in business terms and talk the language of business. We must be able to resource training not just from within but by using the vast array of external resources. We must be able to manage our activities as well as any other manager. We must share in the creation and communication of the company's vision. We must never let the goals of the company out of our sight.

In short, we may have to grow and change with the business. It will be hard. We shall have to demonstrate not only relevance but also value for money and achievement of results. We shall be our own boss, as accountable for results as any other line manager, and we shall have to deal with fewer internal resources.

The challenge is on, as many T&D specialists have demonstrated to me over the past few years. We need to be capable of meeting that challenge. This is why McGraw-Hill Publishing Company have planned and launched this major new training series—to help us meet that challenge.

The series covers all aspects of T&D and provides the knowledge base from which we can develop plans to meet the challenge. They are practical books for the professional person. They are a starting point for planning our journey into the twenty-first century.

Use them well. Don't just read them. Highlight key ideas, thoughts, action pointers or whatever, and have a go at doing something with them. Through experimentation we evolve; through stagnation we die.

I know that all the authors in the McGraw-Hill Training Series would want me to wish you good luck. Have a great journey into the twenty-first century.

ROGER BENNETT
Series Editor

About the series editor

Roger Bennett has over 20 years' experience in training, management education, research and consulting. He has long been involved with trainer training and trainer effectiveness. He has carried out research into trainer effectiveness, and conducted workshops, seminars, and conferences on the subject around the world. He has written extensively on the subject including the book *Improving Trainer Effectiveness*, Gower. His work has taken him all over the world and has involved directors of companies as well as managers and trainers.

Dr Bennett has worked in engineering, several business schools (including the International Management Centre, where he launched the UK's first master's degree in T&D), and has been a board director of two companies. He is the editor of the *Journal of European Industrial Training* and was series editor of the ITD's *Get In There* workbook and video package for the managers of training departments. He now runs his own business called The Management Development Consultancy.

Acknowledgements

I would like to acknowledge the contribution others have made to the material in this book: firstly, those who have offered me effective workplace and non-workplace counselling, and helped me to begin to recognize the difference it could make to my development; secondly, those who have been the recipients of my workplace counselling, and allowed me to learn and develop those skills and qualities for myself; thirdly, those who have undergone workplace counselling training with me, and helped me to continue to develop a comprehensive and useful package through their feedback and suggestions; and, fourthly, my 'support network' through the years, who have maintained my enthusiasm and stimulated new ideas and approaches.

I would also like to acknowledge the helpfulness of Ian Deamer in reading and commenting on part of the draft manuscript, the reviewers who gave helpful comments to refine the text, and the editor in dealing with the nitty gritty of turning this into a published work.

Finally, I would like to acknowledge the patient transference of manuscript to word-processor undertaken by John Hume and his unfailing support as I devoted this part of my life to thinking about, worrying about and writing this book.

Di Kamp

Preface

Any good 'people' managers have been using basic counselling skills with their staff. This book provides the framework for supporting those managers and enabling them to develop those skills. It also offers a description of how to enable other managers to develop basic counselling skills, so that they can offer similar care for their staff.

The approach which is suggested has been proven to be useful in practice. It is the basis on which I have worked with managers, and those in personnel functions, who have responsibility for helping to develop staff. Much of the approach is based on the principles of Neuro Linguistic Programming—the study of excellence—and several of the techniques included will be recognizable to anyone who has studied NLP.

It is not easy to separate out the skills of counselling from the other skills of a good 'people' manager. Whenever a manager is dealing directly with his or her staff, there is likely to be some element of counselling involved. The distinction comes in the intended outcome of the particular interaction.

With coaching and training, the outcome is guided by the manager and he or she expects a particular end result. None the less, there may be a counselling element within the coaching or training situation. When the outcome is that the person concerned explores their own issue and comes to their own conclusion or decision, then there is counselling.

This overlap of different skills could lead to difficulties in separating out the particular part called counselling. On the other hand, it reinforces the importance of developing counselling skills. If they are inherent in so many interactions, then they are a crucial area for professional development.

My intention throughout the book is to provide useful material for any trainer who is enabling managers to develop their skills. Parts 1 and 2 set the context and give definition to the distinction of workplace counselling. Parts 3 to 5 describe the approach to take in the actual training of the managers.

Just as some managers have already developed their workplace counselling skills, so you as a trainer will already have considered some of the points I will make in this book. I hope that it will offer you a different perspective as well as reinforcing what you already know.

It is intended to provide you with a reference point, rather than just something to read. Having read the book through, I hope that you will use it to dip into when you want to re-examine particular aspects, or explore particular avenues. It also contains some activities which you can use or adapt within your own training.

I have enjoyed and learnt from the process of putting this book together. I hope that you will find it both stimulating and useful in your work with workplace counsellors.

Di Kamp

PART ONE

The changing workplace

This part provides the context within which training in workplace counselling will take place. It will give you the background information which relates this training to current and future business needs in a general sense.

1 Putting people first

The number of organizations which now state that people are their most important resource, through mission statements, value statements, and so on, grows day by day.

This is a major change from the 'profits first' mentality which has been predominant in business for as long as anyone can remember. It is a change which is long overdue and suggests that common sense may be beginning to permeate the business world.

Reasons for change

When organizations were competing on a local level, then changing the product or the equipment could result in the short-term advantage required. The people involved either adapted or were replaced.

Now competition is global, and technology is readily available to many rather than the few. With the improved communications links world-wide, the global infrastructures for moving goods and services quickly, and the speed with which new ideas can be developed and promulgated, it is more difficult to stay ahead of the game.

Just look at the cars on the road now. They originate from a vast range of countries, and come in an enormous variety of shapes, sizes, colours and capacities. To be competitive in this field, as in any other, requires a more sophisticated understanding of what makes the difference.

The competitive edge

All organizations want the competitive edge. Even those which have traditionally been sole providers of a service, such as public sector organizations, are now beginning to find that there are alternatives being offered to their services from the private sector.

The consumer is also more sophisticated. We have been educated to expect certain standards of quality and variety as consumers, and are now more discriminating in our choice. 'Brand loyalty' is now less certain. If something is better than our previous preference, we are now more likely to choose on merit, rather than loyalty.

Achieving quality   The ability to offer consistent and continually improving quality of product or service is an obvious area to look for the competitive edge. However much organizations improve the efficiency of their processes and methods, they will still only be effective if the people who are working with them are committed to quality and the search for continued improvement.

People do not lack a desire to improve quality or to give of their best. There is a great sense of pride in being associated with the production of an excellent service or product. Frequently, however, they feel that the workplace does not care enough to make it worth their while to use their talents and commitment. In fact, the opposite may be true—they may feel that the way they are treated in the workplace de-motivates them.

Attempts to improve quality through processes, without fully engaging the people involved in a commitment to quality, have not produced the results required. This therefore forces organizations to re-consider the way in which they manage their employees, so that they will be committed to quality. They need to find ways to harness and channel the motivation and commitment of their employees so that they are engaged.

Being innovative   The other important area to look for the competitive edge is through innovation. This can be at two levels: innovation in methods, and innovation in product.

Innovation in methods   Improving the method of producing a product or service is widely recognized to be an essential in today's changing world. The large-scale improvements which can be made are now rapidly available across the range of organizations, and so give no particular competitive edge. It is the smaller-scale continuous improvements to efficiency and effectiveness which make the difference, on the whole.

At this level, it is not the research and development expert who will spot the possibilities, but the person who is working with the process.

Anyone who has spent time talking with people about their jobs is likely to have heard some comments about how the job could be done more effectively. Yet these ideas have either not been offered up to the organization, or have not been taken seriously.

To encourage people to offer these ideas, organizations need to demonstrate that they value employees' opinions, and want and will use the ideas.

Joan worked in the postal section of a large company. She realized that a slight reorganization of the post-room would significantly speed up the distribution procedure, at little cost to the company.

When she proposed it to her manager, he told her it was his job to think of ways of improving the service, and she should concentrate on getting on with her job. Joan was one of the most cynical when asked to attend a training workshop on empowerment.

Innovation in product

There have been whole departments in some organizations devoted to thinking up new products. This has actually focused creativity into one particular area, and ignored the wealth of creativity in the rest of the organization.

With the increased demand for novelty and variety among consumers, there is obvious sense in beginning to tap into the creativity of all employees. What is more, the wider range of experience and contacts often brings more useful ideas. For example, the salesperson will often register the potential for a different product, before the research department does, through the constant contact with customers. And the assembly worker who knows that he or she would be more tempted to buy the product being assembled if it were smaller, or more brightly coloured, or differently packaged has the advantage of consumer perspective.

Tapping into innovation

To call on the innovative and creative abilities of employees requires more than just the mechanisms to do so. Suggestion schemes were established by a lot of organizations, as they realized that this potential was an important resource which could help them achieve the competitive edge. After an initial burst of enthusiasm, many suggestion schemes fall by the wayside. This is not because of a finite limit to the number of ideas employees have, but because they need to feel that they are valued before they will continue to offer their ideas for improvements.

Valuing people

Organizations which want to succeed in a changing world now need to recognize that their most valuable asset is their people. It is the personal commitment, motivation and innovation of their staff which will give them the competitive edge over others.

Making the statement is the first step in acknowledging this important change in emphasis in working practice. It is, however, only the first step. To be convinced, employees need much more than a statement.

The need for evidence

For most employees, work has not been a source of self-esteem, satisfaction of potential, or feeling valued. The number of people who 'come alive' when describing their garden, their involvement with a local community group, or their social activities, as opposed to their work, far outweigh those who enthuse about their job.

When an organization declares its policy to be putting people first, these employees are likely to greet the statement with scepticism. Their previous experience of work suggests to them that it is unlikely to be more than an empty promise. Furthermore, most organizations have been going through a process of so-called re-structuring. From the employee's perspective, this just looks like getting rid of people— hardly an illustration of putting people first!

To counteract this scepticism, the organization needs to give some pretty strong evidence that it means what it says.

Working practice

This evidence has to be embedded throughout the working practice. It is not enough to introduce suggestion schemes, health care, social events and so on.

All these rely on people's attitudes to them. If the manner in which they are administered does not reinforce the intention of demonstrating that people are valued, they do not have the desired effect. So we come back to *people* making the difference. The people in this instance are the managers and supervisors who lead in the installing of new policies.

Everyday behaviour

These managers are, whether they like it or not, the exemplars of what valuing people looks like in practice. They have the responsibility of modelling a way of managing people which demonstrates that people are valued, not just by the way in which they implement organizational policies, but also in the everyday interactions which they have with their staff.

Dealing with the whole person

This need to demonstrate that people are valued in the organization goes further than just valuing the work they do, and the capabilities they have.

Historical perspective

This was recognized over a century ago by the Quaker employers, who provided housing and welfare for their employees, and made great efforts to ensure that their workforce was cared for. They realized that the returns in terms of loyalty and commitment made it worth their while.

Nowadays, such complete provision for employees would be seen, quite rightly, as paternalistic. Employees are more likely to prefer to have the right to choose for themselves, rather than be looked after in such a manner. It would also be unrealistic. We no longer have jobs for life, and that form of 'cradle to grave' provision is inappropriate.

Present-day application It is still relevant, however, to offer services which help the human being, rather than just the employee. The principle of recognizing that people's experience of life outside work will affect how they are inside work still applies.

Organizational level

Offering health care and facilities for maintaining fitness helps to maintain a healthy workforce. Having banks and shops on site gives recognition to the need for people to run their everyday lives as well. Having a subsidized restaurant with high quality food encourages people to eat properly. Laying on educational facilities can enable people to develop themselves in ways which they choose. Recognizing that people may need career breaks, time off for important family events, etc., acknowledges that they have other priorities in life besides work which may need to be catered for.

All these give recognition to the whole person and are effective in helping to give evidence that the people matter.

Individual level

This organizational message then has to be translated into an everyday working level.

The evidence that counts here is very powerful and very simple: knowing people's names; knowing something of their personal circumstances; allowing them to bring personal touches into the workplace; treating them as fellow human beings.

Here again, it is the managers and supervisors who bear the brunt of giving the evidence that they value the whole person. It is they who set the tone for what happens in the workplace.

EVIDENCE THAT PEOPLE ARE GENUINELY VALUED

- Installing relevant policies with commitment
- Managing people with respect
- Offering services to meet the everyday needs of employees
- Giving educational opportunities
- Allowing for career breaks and family commitments
- Recognizing the individuality of people.

The obstacles to putting people first

What I have described so far surely makes sense. People *are* what makes the difference to success in an organization. In order to get the results wanted from people, the organization needs to demonstrate that they are valued, in ways which impact on the people. Why, then, is there not a common recognition that putting people first is obvious and normal working practice?

Short-term objectives

While recognizing the business need to demonstrate that people come first, organizations are still caught up by short-term business objectives. Profitability and productivity still tend to be measured against short-term targets, and govern the extent to which people can be put first.

The approaches and behaviours which value people are often put on one side until the targets have been met, and the two objectives of the organization—profitability and valuing people—are often seen as conflicting demands, rather than there being true recognition that valuing people leads to profitability.

The history of working practice

It has not been normal practice to care for and value people at work. We have all absorbed the belief that workplaces exploit people and do not use their full potential. To change this requires more than a laid-down set of behaviours. It demands a change to our own beliefs about work. This means that there has to be powerful evidence that valuing people does work, and powerful evidence for the employees that they are being valued.

Overcoming the obstacles

It is the heads of organizations who have to find a way through the apparently conflicting demands of valuing people and making profits. There are examples now in existence: The Body Shop, Virgin and Semco are three large organizations which demonstrate that valuing people can lead to profitability.

At the level of working practice, we can all play our part. As trainers, we can make a difference both by treating people differently ourselves, and by enabling managers to develop the skills they need to be able to be the models of working practice that are now required.

Key points

- Organizations now have a business need to value people in their organizations.
- Competitive edge is gained through continuous improvement in quality and innovation.
- Quality and innovation come from the people in the organization.
- To gain this competitive edge, organizations have to prove that they value their people.
- They give this proof at an organizational level through schemes and facilities.
- At an individual level it requires managers to treat people differently.
- Obstacles to this change include the history of working practice, and the apparent conflict between profitability and valuing people.
- The change in working practice will come when organizations recognize that profitability follows from valuing people and managers are actively encouraged to develop their people skills.

2 The changing role of managers and personnel

In Chapter 1, I pointed out that managers are crucial to embedding the valuing of people as normal working practice. Pity the poor managers! From their perspective, this is just one more burden laid on their shoulders.

The problems caused by the conflict between significant changes happening in the organizational world, and the leftovers from previous ways of working all seem to centre on the management role.

Historical perspective

Managers have been traditionally expected to control their staff, make sure that they did their work, and generally keep them in line.

Furthermore, many managers have been neglected in terms of training for their new role. They have been good at what they were doing, and promoted to management, without proper preparation and development for the difference in function.

They have therefore learnt how to be managers by following the example of those who managed them, thus perpetuating the management by control model.

Even those who have been given the opportunity to develop their management skills through some form of training are often pulled away from their attempts to do something different by the strength of the traditional way of managing within the workplace. This can be seen both in peer group pressure, and in pressure from their employees, who expect the manager to fulfil the role as they see it, even if that form of management does not motivate them.

It is both sad and comical that the same employees who complained about the autocratic manager who treated them like idiots will equally complain when they have a new manager who asks them for their opinion!

Structural changes

In more recent years, the tendency in most organizations has been to 'streamline' the structure. While the principle behind this tendency is sound, in practice it has often resulted in considerable extra pressure on managers.

The theory of streamlining an organizational structure is linked to the empowerment of employees, so that more and more decision-making is devolved to those most affected by the decision. By devolving decision-making, the need for an extended chain of command no longer exists, and so the structure can be flatter and slimmer, and therefore more effective and flexible.

In practice, streamlining and empowerment have often not gone hand in hand in organizations. Many organizations have used the streamlining as a way of dealing with the short-term economic necessity of reducing costs, without really considering the implications long term.

What is more, proportionately more managerial positions disappear than at any other level.

Effect on managers

These structural changes, without the consequent shift in management style, result in overstressed and overworked managers.

I can think of one example of a manager who told me that his job was now more fulfilling because his people made the decisions and ran the area, and he supported and encouraged them, delighting in watching their skills and abilities develop.

I can think of hundreds of managers who have expressed to me their feeling of being overloaded, of having twice or three times as much to control now. What is worse, they feel that they *have* to be seen to be working long hours and holding on to decision-making, because otherwise they may be the next to be made redundant.

Demands of the role

Besides being expected to manage larger numbers as an effect of streamlining the organizational structure, managers are also being asked to take on other responsibilities which have traditionally rested elsewhere.

The workplace counsellor is one such responsibility. There is also that of assessor of competency, and trainer. For most managers, these just look like additional burdens, because the pressures of command and control have not been removed.

They can also be seen as causing conflict in the demands of the role. When the manager is expected to discipline his or her employees, make them work hard, and at the same time counsel them and encourage their development, it can lead to considerable difficulty for that individual.

> Phil, a manager in a large company, was upset by his results in the upward appraisal system. His staff said that he was actively discouraging them from developing themselves, and that he was only supportive when they met their targets. He pointed out that he was under considerable pressure to meet targets, and could not afford to have staff diverted from that to work on their own development, however much he liked the idea. He would immediately be in trouble from his line manager if he said that they had not met targets because staff were on development programmes. Yet now he was receiving a dressing-down for complying with this pressure.

Personnel staff

It is important to include personnel staff here because they are the ones who have traditionally provided workplace counselling. Their role, too, is changing, and they may also find it hard to adjust.

Historical perspective

Historically, personnel has been a distinct function which dealt with recruitment, welfare, industrial relations and similar associated responsibilities.

Although some of the personnel function has been purely administrative, there has been an ethos of concern and care for the individual. This has sometimes put them at odds with the core business, where they have been seen as 'too soft'. They have often been a 'poor relation' in terms of influence, and seen as a necessary evil rather than an important part of the business. However, they were a useful referral point for 'problems' with staff, whether sent by managers, or choosing to go themselves.

Structural changes

The streamlining of organizations has included in most cases a re-definition of the personnel function.

For some, this has just meant a change of title, to Human Resources! For most, this new title has brought with it an increase in responsibilities as numbers in departments have been reduced.

There is also a growing trend to attach personnel staff to particular areas of the core business rather than keep them separate. While this may offer the chance to be more influential in how the business works, it makes many personnel staff feel more vulnerable and isolated.

Demands of the role

Personnel staff are now more likely to be asked to fulfil a variety of personnel functions, rather than to specialize in one area.

They are also, if placed into the core business, having to manage the conflict between their criteria for personnel care, and the drive to get the job done in the core business. For most, there will have been little in the way of training to help them deal with this changing role.

At the same time, they can see some of their role being taken away from them, as managers are being asked to take on more responsibility for their employees.

Effect on personnel staff The effect of all this on personnel staff will vary, depending on how exactly their role has changed in the particular organization.

- Some will be feeling threatened and put out of a job.
- Some will be feeling vulnerable, and unsure of their ability to fulfil their new role.
- Some will be confused as to what they should hold as their values in dealing with people.

The need for clarification

As organizations begin to get hold of the implications of becoming a changing and learning organization, they will need to clarify the changing roles and responsibilities of their staff.

The trend for managers It is fairly evident that 'control and command' management will not work within the changed structure and ethos of organizations. It leads to overload for the managers, and a lack of empowerment for their employees.

Managers have to learn how to let go of the reins of decision-making, and take on the role of leader: inspiring, motivating and supporting their staff in achieving the results required. This is a major shift of emphasis, and is not achieved simply by saying it has to happen.

Valuing the changed role It is vital that organizations recognize this shift of emphasis by giving evidence that they value these behaviours in managers.

This means that the behaviours need to be prevalent in role descriptions, selection procedures, appraisal frameworks, and development opportunities.

Making it possible At the same time, it is important to enable managers to let go of some of the existing demands caused by the transition from the traditional style. This means that they need help in letting go of the control, and their staff need help in learning how to take on appropriate responsibility for their own work results.

Personnel staff Although not as complex as the managerial role, in terms of change, none the less, there is also a major shift of emphasis for personnel staff.

They will, more and more, be expected to offer generic personnel skills, and to place those directly in the business context, as part of a team. The reasoning behind this change needs to be made clear, and recognition needs to be given to the development requirements of these staff if they are to fulfil the role well.

Where are you up to?

Every organization I deal with is at a different stage in the transition from a traditional to a learning organization. The majority of organizations are still struggling with how to change the management style, how to demonstrate they value people, how to re-define roles so people work smarter, how to maintain profitability while making the changes necessary for maintaining their success long-term. Wherever your organization is on the continuum of transition, it is likely that staff need help in coming to terms with and making sense of the changes.

We are not talking about minor adjustments in roles and functions. We are talking about major re-definition. It does not happen overnight, and people do not let go of old habits easily.

Yet the changes are necessary and inevitable, and our role as trainers in enabling those changes to happen is crucial.

Key points

- Managers are now being expected to change from control management to leadership. Problems in making this change include:
  — strength of traditional ways of working;
  — increase in workload;
  — still being expected to take control as well as play new role;
  — fear of not seeming busy enough;
  — lack of training for new responsibilities.

- Personnel staff are now being expected to have generic skills and work directly in the core business. Problems in making this change include:
  — managing the possible clash in values;
  — lack of training for extended skills required;
  — fear of their role disappearing altogether.

- Organizations need to clarify the changed roles for both, and ensure that they are valued for their new skills.
- They also need to offer appropriate training for the changed roles, and for the employees who also have a changed role.
- While in transition, there is need for help and direction, and recognition of some of the problems.

3 The changing role of the trainer

Many of the issues that I have already identified for managers and personnel staff in a changing organization are also issues for trainers.

We too are caught up in the transition, and are facing uncertainty about our role. It is up to us to decide to take the lead in helping to ease the transition for ourselves and for others. By doing so, we forge ourselves a clear and vital role within any organization.

Historical perspective

Originally, trainers were those who passed on their own highly developed skills to others who needed to develop those skills. They were primarily instructors who did their best to use their expertise to teach others. There are still trainers in organizations for whom this was their route into training.

Training developed into a separate profession when it was recognized that there are specific skills involved in communicating information and helping people to enhance their abilities.

Most of us are training specialists with qualifications, and have been recognized for both our subject knowledge and our training abilities. This recognition has generally been given through requests for us to organize training events to meet the training needs identified within the organization. The equation of the training role with designing and implementing what you might call 'stand alone' training courses has held true for a long time, and still exists in many organizations.

Trainer development

Trainer development has tended to confirm this view of training and has only recently adjusted to give more emphasis to the enabling of learning, with the much broader implications for the trainer's role which that entails.

Some trainers have recognized that for their training to be effective, it needs to have an impact on the business, and involves much more than just doing training courses. However, they have often found that the organization was not ready to accept a different approach. Now, though, the pressure is on to take training into the twenty-first century.

The pressures for change

Whether, as trainers, we were already wanting to make changes or not, we now have little choice in the matter. The radical changes in the world of work impinge on our role, just as they do on those of others.

Structural change

Slimming of organizations includes a close examination of training departments. Where there is no perceived intrinsic value to the organization in having such a department, the whole function may be out-sourced.

Where training departments survive, they are expected to make a clear and valuable contribution to the business, with their work linked to business objectives, and an evaluation process which demonstrates that their work is making a difference in the workplace.

Role re-definitions

There is the additional pressure created by the different responsibilities now being taken on by managers. More and more, they are expected to identify the development needs of their staff, and to take on the role of coach in helping that development. This puts into question the previously accepted view of the trainer as the training specialist.

Although these pressures may seem to indicate that the trainer is a dying species, in fact, they may be just what we need to bring the role of the trainer into a more useful and valued position in the organization.

What do we have to offer?

As trainers, we have spent our professional lives developing ways of helping others to learn. Both during the transition phase in organizational change, and in the newly developing organizational culture, learning is the most important skill anyone can have. Many organizations are now calling themselves learning organizations, and this recognizes the fact that the future is no longer predictable, so we all need to be on a journey of continuous learning and development.

To achieve this, everyone needs to learn how they learn best. As trainers, we can offer invaluable help and guidance in developing learning skills.

How do we offer this?

To begin with we need to re-define our role to that of enabler of learning. This is important for our own development—we need to move away from being the expert who teaches others, and towards the role of someone who is expert at facilitating a learning process. The re-definition will also help us to carve out the niche within the organization where we can be of most benefit to the business. Training keeps us away from the core of the business, whereas enabling learning is central to a learning organization.

To help develop learning skills, we need to work with people, not just on courses, but also out in the workplace. This gives us the opportunity to become intrinsically valuable to the organization, coaching and facilitating learning inside the work environment.

We can also use our training skills to enable others to help their staff develop their learning skills. By training others to take on the development of learning skills, we enhance our ability to influence what happens.

The benefits Instead of being squeezed out of the training role, we can take it to a different level, and play an important part in helping the organization to be successful in a changing world.

As we are talking about major changes in working practice, we will need to support and reinforce strongly the different approach to learning, so as to embed it in the organizational culture.

What else can we do? As the development of continuous learning takes hold, we can add in two other qualities which professional trainers are likely to be aware of: the importance of modelling good practice; and the constant need for innovation.

Modelling good practice We have the opportunity as trainers to set the example of how people need to behave to achieve the change in working practice.

We can be examples of how to enable learning in others—we do that already. We can also demonstrate in our everyday behaviour how to value people and how to be a continuous learner. For many of us, this gives us the opportunity to free ourselves from the role of expert and the artificial pressures which that creates. Instead we become the partner of the learner, helping them and learning ourselves at the same time.

There are not enough models of a different way of working, and we can provide significant value in taking on this role.

Being innovative Finally, we can enjoy our own creative potential, and contribute our ability to innovate to the growth of the organization.

By experimenting with different approaches to enabling learning, by contributing our different perspective to business issues, we increase our usefulness to the organization. At the same time, we increase our involvement in the business and help ourselves to realize more of our potential.

It is up to us to re-create our role, and to make the part we play in the changing organization a valuable one, for us, for those we work with, and for the organization as a whole.

By being ready for change ourselves, we can more easily support and help others as they try to cope with the problems of transition.

The remainder of this book is designed to help you to make the change. It offers an approach to training workplace counsellors which exemplifies the way we need to work in a change organization.

Key points

- The training function is under pressure from organizational re-structuring and from the devolution of more training responsibility to managers.
- Trainers can use their professional experience to forge a new role for themselves.
- They can concentrate on developing learning skills.
- They can help managers to develop the learning skills of their staff.
- They can be exemplars of new working practice.
- They can be innovative.
- Trainers will benefit by the broader use of their potential.
- They will add more value to the organization as a whole.
- They can support others during the transition.

PART TWO

What are counselling skills?

In Part 2 we will define what is meant by workplace counselling, how it is useful, and where it is appropriate to use it. This will enable you to clarify in your own mind what you will be offering in your training, so that your customers are clear about what they are committing to, and what its value to them will be.

4 The workplace counsellor

If we are to offer useful and effective training to managers and personnel staff, we need to take account of the changing context in which all of us are working.

Having looked at some of the issues which arise because of changes in organizational practice, we now need to define carefully what exactly we are training these people to do.

It is very easy to get enthused by the idea of training people to be counsellors, and lose sight of the distinctions between professional counselling and workplace counselling.

As trainers, we need to be aware of the difference between the profession of counselling, and the application of first-line counselling skills in the workplace. This distinction affects how we approach counselling skills development in two ways:

1 It makes us aware of how the professional counsellor image may prevent managers and personnel staff from wanting to be trained in counselling.
2 It helps us to design training programmes which are realistic and useful in meeting the real needs of our clients, and their staff.

Professional counselling

Professional counselling is a specialized profession. It requires years of training and a careful supervision of the practice of the skills counselling. Professional counsellors have a specific function. They provide in-depth support to people who are wanting to deal with crises or to make changes in their lives. Their clients choose to attend, and commit to working with them until the client feels that the issues have been resolved. Being a counsellor is their job, not a part of their role.

It is no wonder that managers and personnel staff feel that they cannot be a counsellor!

The counselling image

Being a counsellor carries with it a particular image. This consists of several elements which do not seem to fit with what people are expected to do and be at work, particularly in a busy and changing environment.

Personal qualities   Counselling tends to be associated with someone who is very caring with patient qualities. There is also a sense of the 'do-gooder' about counselling. We see counsellors as people who put others first and are unselfish. This may extend into seeing counsellors as 'soft'. Managers may well question if they have enough of these qualities.

Most managers do not perceive that they were selected because they are nice people who demonstrate a 'soft' approach to others. The personal qualities that they feel that they have been valued for are more likely to be in the area of getting things done: being organized, and task-driven. They may also wish to project a stronger image to their staff, and believe that the apparent emphasis of these 'counselling' qualities would detract from their perceived effective leadership.

Susan feels that she had to be tough to achieve management status in a historically male environment. Her work persona is authoritative, and she is known to be someone who gets the work done. Her staff are somewhat in awe of her, and certainly would not see her as a 'counsellor'.

She fears that if she lets her gentler, more caring side show, she will lose control over her staff. They may like her better, but will they work as hard?

These more caring characteristics are facets of ourselves which have not been traditionally part of our workplace persona, and as I described earlier, the apparent conflict between demonstrating these personal qualities, and the need to drive hard to achieve targets still exists in the minds of many.

Principles   Attached to counselling is a principle of non-directiveness. This implies listening impartially, without judging or leading. In the workplace, this may seem inappropriate.

The manager or personnel officer often has a specific result in mind when they see someone for counselling. Even if the person has asked to see the manager or personnel officer, the latter's prime intention in listening is likely to be to get the person back to working effectively. This intention seems to contradict the principle of non-directiveness.

Further, the professional counsellor's approach is based entirely on the individual and his or her needs which may seem inappropriate in a workplace setting, where the needs of the team or the company will also have to be taken into account.

Time It is generally accepted that going to see a counsellor means a series of regular counselling sessions which can go on for months or even years before you really get the problem sorted out, and each session typically lasts at least half an hour, often longer.

A manager or personnel officer has many responsibilities and an already impossible workload. To accept the role of counsellor would necessitate finding much more time to give to individuals, and that just does not seem possible, even if they want to.

PERCEIVED OBSTACLES IN MANAGERS BEING COUNSELLORS

- The 'soft' personal qualities required may detract from the strong image of managers.
- The manager needs to get people to work effectively, and may not be impartial about results.
- The individual's needs may have to be subsumed under company or team needs.
- There is not enough time to spare

The workplace counsellor

It is important to acknowledge that the manager as counsellor is not trying to replace the professional counsellor.

When we talk about the workplace counsellor, we are looking at first-line counselling, as part of management and personnel skills. Most people will not need the services of a professional counsellor in their lives. Yet all of us will have appreciated someone who has 'been there' for us when we needed some help or someone just to listen. These people are ordinary people, just like us—in fact, we have all probably been on both sides of this type of interaction.

What first-line counselling can offer is qualities and skills which most of us have, potentially. It is more like the everyday interactions described above than professional counselling.

Meaning of counsellor

If we go back to the meaning of the word 'counsellor', before it became the title for a profession, we discover it means someone to discuss with, plan with, deliberate with. If we revert to that description of a counsellor, it is easy to identify the personal qualities and it becomes more useful from the point of view of the manager or personnel officer.

It is also important to notice that these qualities are within most of us. They are not exceptional or special, in that most of us have demonstrated them some of the time in our lives. The difference is in giving the demonstration of these qualities value as part of the role of the manager or personnel officer.

Chaucer offered the advice: 'Take no counsel from a fool.' We are all foolish sometimes, but with workplace counsellors we want to bring out the qualities in them which make them someone that a person would choose to deliberate, discuss and plan with.

It is useful to remember that in our personal lives we are quite comfortable with showing a range of qualities and behaviours, depending on the situation.

> As a parent, I may be the disciplinarian when my child behaves badly, the teacher when my child gets his or her first bike, the sympathetic friend when my child is upset because a friend has fallen out with him or her, and the counsellor when my child is anxious about starting a new school. We do not consider this to be inconsistent, but rather to be good parenting.

In the same way, managers and personnel officers now need to let go of the traditional 'persona' in the workplace, and use their full range of skills and behaviours appropriately, according to the situation. Training in workplace counselling is therefore about highlighting the conscious use of relevant qualities and skills, in appropriate situations, as a part of the range of skills and behaviours which are used at work. We are developing this area of human behaviour in managers and personnel staff to enable them to be more effective in their dealings with others, with more options of how to react in the workplace.

DEFINITION OF WORKPLACE COUNSELLING

The workplace counsellor is anyone who offers useful support to others, in a one-to-one situation, to help them to be more effective.

This support can range from being a sounding board to exploring solutions through to giving specific advice or practical help.

Personal qualities When in a counselling situation, the personal qualities which make the difference are most easily identified as those which a friend demonstrates when you sit and talk to them.

Approachability The use of the example of a friend reminds us that the person needs to be approachable for someone even to consider using them as a counsellor.

There needs to be some rapport, and the person being counselled needs to feel comfortable in the counsellor's presence. This does not mean that it has to be a long-standing relationship—after all, many people have told their life story to strangers on trains! But there does need to be a sense that the person is friendly, will not judge you, and that you are valued as an individual, so that you will not feel that you are just being a nuisance.

Concern If someone makes you feel you can approach them, then the next quality is obvious concern and interest in your well-being. If you need some help, you want someone who cares, and cares in a healthy encouraging way. You need to feel that someone else wants you to feel better, or even better about yourself and your life. This does not necessarily mean that the person is 'soft'. In fact sometimes it is downright annoying to have someone say 'Oh dear!' or 'What a shame!', when you really want to be helped to see things differently.

Attention It is important that the counsellor can put aside other priorities for the time the person is with them and give that person undivided attention. Most of us can listen attentively, although we may not think we are good listeners. Again, the example of listening to friends and family springs to mind. When it is 'important', for us or for them, we do it. So the workplace counsellor needs to find what makes it important enough to pay attention (see Chapter 5).

Wisdom When you look for someone to counsel you, you want the counsellor to have some wisdom. This does not necessarily mean that they are clever, or know the answer. It does mean that they will respond and react in a considered way, and contribute something useful.

Notice that the wisdom is not linked necessarily to age or qualifications. I have sometimes found more wisdom in a child's comments than in those of the adults I talked to!

Wisdom also implies that the issue has been taken seriously. The person being counselled does not want a flippant or dismissive response.

Integrity The individual needs to feel that the person they are talking to has integrity. In this context, it means that the individual feels that the counsellor can be trusted to treat what is said with respect, and to treat it as confidential, unless permission is given to talk about it with others.

It also implies that the counsellor will be honest with you. You do not want the counsellor to pretend to agree with you, just to shut you up, or calm you down. Nor do you want them to keep information from you which may affect the results you want.

PERSONAL QUALITIES OF A WORKPLACE COUNSELLOR

- Approachability: making someone feel comfortable.
- Concern: genuine interest in someone's well-being.
- Attention: giving importance to the issue.

- Wisdom: considered reaction.
- Integrity: respect and confidentiality.

These personal qualities encompass others and to some extent overlap. They can really be summarized by saying that they are the qualities of someone you would be glad to take advice from.

Principles of workplace counselling

Some of the principles attached to professional counselling may well be inappropriate in the workplace. It is important to acknowledge the different context in which the workplace counsellor will be operating.

However, there are principles which are appropriate and necessary as a prerequisite for engaging in workplace counselling. They are similar to those in professional counselling, but adapted to fit the context of the workplace.

Results

It is vital to recognize that workplace counselling has the intention of improving performance, directly or indirectly. This can take a variety of forms, for example:

- Helping someone to find a way of speeding up their job.
- Dealing with persistent absenteeism.
- Helping someone to find a way to deal with personal issues more effectively, so that work performance is not affected.
- Helping someone to identify that they are in the wrong job, and how to find the right job.
- Dealing with low self-esteem and helping to raise confidence.
- Dealing with issues around work relationships.
- Looking at potential career development.
- Conducting a staff appraisal interview.

If there is no difference in performance, then the counselling has not been effective. And this intention is implicit to both sides of the counselling.

The employee may choose or be asked to talk with their manager about an issue. Even if it is something personal, there is an expectation that he or she will help to find a way to manage it better in the workplace primarily, although the employee may also hope that the manager will help them find a way to deal with the issue in their private life.

Client-centredness

The solutions arrived at through counselling need to be suited to the client, rather than the counsellor's view of what is right. This is an obvious principle in professional counselling, and relatively easy to fulfil, in that the only obstacle would be the counsellor's personal point of view, and the counsellor is trained to deal with the tendency to put a personal slant on their responses.

However, the same principle applies in workplace counselling because it has the intention of resulting in an improvement in performance, whether initiated by the manager or personnel officer or by the person they are talking to. This effect will only be achieved if the person can commit themselves wholeheartedly to the conclusions reached. So the workplace counsellor also needs to work with the person they are talking to until a strategy is found which the person can own and take on personally. Although the reason for being client-centred may be different, the effect is similar.

Confidentiality   Even if the professional counsellor were to discuss a client's problems with others, the likelihood is that you would never know. In the workplace, confidentiality is vital. The person needs to be sure that anything said will 'stay within these four walls' if they are to really feel safe in exploring an issue. Not only is there the issue of the 'grapevines' of workplaces being notorious for spreading leaks of information and/or rumour, there is also the issue of repercussions. If what someone tells the manager about their feelings towards a colleague might get back to that colleague, then most people will avoid the danger of adverse reactions.

By giving this safety to an employee, the manager or personnel officer is more likely to find out what the real issues are, and therefore be able to help to find solutions which work, rather than cosmetic ones.

PRINCIPLES OF WORKPLACE COUNSELLING

- Results: there is an improvement in performance.
- Client-centred: the conclusions/actions suit the individual.
- Confidentiality: ensuring that the person feels safe in discussing the real issue.

The principles of workplace counselling are not so different from those of a professional counsellor, but they do need to be adjusted to fit the particular context.

Time for counselling   Finally, there is the question of time given to counselling. Time is a major issue for most managers and personnel staff. Even if they want to offer workplace counselling to their staff, and they have or can develop the skills and qualities required, they may feel that there is insufficient time to devote to this part of their role, particularly if they view workplace counselling as on a par with professional counselling.

Here it is important to remember that the workplace counsellor is only offering first-line counselling. The intention is not to help people sort their lives out, it is to effect an improvement in performance.

If someone has major personal issues to sort out, then professional help is needed. For most people, however, a small amount of time, where they are given full attention, is enough to help them to make the difference they are looking for. Everyone knows that the manager or personnel officer has lots of other responsibilities to fulfil. It is the quality of time and attention given which makes the difference, rather than the quantity.

Most people are capable of being a workplace counsellor. Some naturally find it easier than others to take on the role. What managers and personnel staff need is a clear definition of what it is, where it applies, and how it will make them more effective in their wider role.

Once that information is in place, then the enhancement of their skills and abilities is a relatively easy task.

Key points

- A workplace counsellor:
  — is approachable;
  — shows genuine concern;
  — gives attention;
  — has wisdom and integrity.
- The principles of workplace counselling are to:
  — have the intention of improving performance;
  — ensure that the solutions suit the client;
  — maintain confidentiality.
- Workplace counselling is the conscious application of skills and behaviours which help people to help themselves improve.

5 Counselling for empowerment

Defining the differences between the professional and the workplace counsellor is only the first step in clarifying what is expected of the manager or personnel officer. This may help to allay their fears that this is a role that they are not capable of taking on, but still leaves the question of why it is worth their while, or valuable to them to enhance their counselling skills.

Unless we can propose that there are obvious benefits for the manager or personnel officer in committing to developing these skills, they will not want to engage in something which they see as bringing them yet more work and responsibility. Workplace counselling needs to be put into context in relation to their overall role, and to the changing demands on them within the organization.

When is it counselling?

It is vital to clarify with managers and personnel staff that workplace counselling is intrinsic to many of their interactions with staff.

It is essentially an approach to interactions which gives the people concerned the opportunity to develop their own solutions. As such, it may be a part of a coaching or training process, a part of a disciplinary process, or a part of normal daily interactions. It does not just apply to the situations where staff need help with a personal problem.

Why use this approach?

In Part 1 of this book, I described the ways in which working practice is changing. A central theme is the importance of valuing people, and finding ways of encouraging and developing their potential. There is beginning to be a pressure to make the changes without much guidance in how to make the difference. We can set workplace counselling skills into this context.

To achieve the changes in working practice, managers and personnel staff need to help staff to learn what being empowered means in practice. There are many complementary approaches to doing this: coaching or training staff in taking on more responsibilities and initiatives; improving processes and structures to enhance empowerment possibilities; using the opportunity of individual interactions to add to the gradual empowerment of their staff through applying the workplace counselling approach.

Workplace counselling can play a part in fulfilling a major business objective: empowering people to become a more valuable resource within the organization.

Even if this is not yet accepted as a major business objective in your organization, you can use the evidence that it is becoming more widespread to encourage people to look ahead and be ready for the development.

What is more, I pointed out in Chapter 1 that there is a lot of cynicism among employees about statements by organizations that they value their people. Employees need some strong evidence that they are valued and cared for as they are, before they will put more of themselves into their work.

Workplace counselling is an excellent way of providing such evidence, because the approach is respectful of the individuals and gives value to their viewpoint. By using this approach to interactions, the managers or personnel officers are laying the foundations for enhancement of the potential of their staff, and demonstrating the change in working practice in action.

What are the benefits to managers and personnel staff?

Unless it seems worth their while, people will be unwilling to invest time and energy in developing their counselling skills. So far we have looked at the potential benefits to the organization as a whole, but this is not enough to convince the hard-pressed manager that he or she should engage in this development. They need to know that their life will be made easier if they bother to develop and use these skills. So, in what ways will they personally benefit?

Understanding of individuals

Firstly, using counselling skills will give them a much better understanding of their staff and what makes them tick. With increased understanding, it is much easier to handle people, because you know the sorts of things which please and motivate them, and can use that knowledge to appeal to them when you need their involvement and commitment.

> By finding out more about Graham, his manager was able to identify that he gained great satisfaction from putting order to things.
>
> The manager then knew exactly who to ask to sort out their chaotic administrative system. Graham was delighted to take it on—it had been irritating him—and he made an excellent job of it.

You also get to know what irritates or upsets them, and this awareness means that you can sometimes stop potential problems happening by ensuring that those situations are avoided which would cause such irritation or upset. Alternatively, the counselling approach can be used to help them to find ways of handling it better.

I would also add that in many cases, getting to know an individual in more depth and understanding their point of view leads to an easier and better working relationship overall. Instead of 'that awkward devil', they often become, 'Fred, who's a bit eccentric in his views'.

Respect from staff The last point works both ways. In the process of counselling, staff also get to know the counsellor better, and often change their attitude towards him or her, because they now appreciate the individual.

This is enhanced in the counselling process, when used well, because the counsellor actively pays attention to the individual, without rushing to judgements or solutions. This type of attention is respectful of the individual, and elicits respect back when it is offered.

The manager or personnel officer is thereby giving evidence of valuing people. Because this is what individuals want and need, the managers will tend to gain respect.

Fewer problems to deal with When counselling skills are used well, the number of problems the manager or personnel officer has to deal with is diminished. This happens in three ways. Firstly, they have less 'repeat' problems. By this I mean those times when they say: 'Sue is up to her old tricks again. I'm going to have to speak to her again. That will give me another two weeks' peace!' By learning to use workplace counselling effectively, they are more likely to resolve the issue first time in a way which works, because the resolution will be created by and owned by the person with the problem.

Secondly, when they use counselling skills effectively, they not only help the person concerned to resolve the immediate issue, they also are informally coaching the person in how to resolve issues for themselves. As people begin to have confidence in their own ability to resolve issues satisfactorily, they take less and less to the workplace counsellor.

Thirdly, the improvement in relationships between the employee and the manager or personnel officer often leads to a reduction in time needing to be spent on problem areas. When there is trust established that they will be taken seriously, staff will often flag up a potential problem long before it becomes a major issue. At this stage it will be much easier to resolve.

More useful time with staff The by-product of a reduction of time spent on problems is that managers and personnel staff can actually enjoy and benefit from time spent with staff. Our relationships with others at work are a large part of our potential job satisfaction, particularly in 'people management' roles. When there are fewer crises, and relationships are pleasant, then job satisfaction increases.

What is more, time spent with staff can be devoted to more satisfying outcomes, like continuing to build the work relationship, and encouraging their development and creativity.

Empowerment of staff

This leads on to the fact that effective counselling will encourage staff to be less dependent on managers, and to take more responsibility for themselves and their workload.

If counselling can contribute to this result, it benefits managers by giving them a strategy for turning the intention of empowerment into action. And as staff do become more empowered, then managers are more able to let go of 'command and control' management, and develop into their own changing role as leader.

Personal development

By developing their counselling skills, managers and personnel officers are actively adding to their own employability. These are skills which can be applied in a whole variety of situations, and will continue to increase in perceived value, because they are a crucial part of empowering others and being a leader.

This form of personal development has the benefits of making the immediate job easier, and of being a part of their development for a changing role. It also frequently has benefits in their personal lives as well. Something which enhances our way of relating to and helping others is as likely to be useful in domestic and social situations as at work.

Finally, through the effective application of skills, workplace counsellors will give themselves the opportunity to learn from others. In my experience, you can learn as much from those you counsel as they do from you: different viewpoints, different ideas, different strategies—and they can all become part of your knowledge and repertoire.

Benefits to the manager and personnel staff

- Greater understanding of the individual's viewpoint, which leads to enhanced ability to motivate them, and improved work relationships.
- Increased respect from their staff.
- Reduction of problems brought to them by their staff.
- More time to spend on development and building positive work relationships.
- Enhanced empowerment of staff.
- More time to lead rather than push.
- Increased personal employability.
- Opportunities to learn and add to their fund of awareness.

These potential benefits for people who develop their counselling skills are important to make explicit. They may seem obvious to those of us who have already experienced the results of effective workplace counselling, but they are not so obvious to the individual who sees counselling as an additional burden of responsibility.

Having established that workplace counselling skills will benefit the manager or personnel officer developing them, we need now to ensure that the other half of the interaction will also benefit.

What difference will it make to employees?

I have already mentioned some of the obvious benefits to employees. They are worth reiterating and spelling out in some detail, because it is essential to the process of counselling that those being counselled have a direct benefit.

Feeling valued

The primary benefit for employees is that they feel valued. The process of workplace counselling puts their interest and their viewpoint first, rather than subsuming them to the interests and viewpoint of the organization or manager.

When you talk to people on the receiving end of enhanced workplace counselling, the most important difference that they notice is that they feel they have been taken notice of, paid attention to, listened to. It is interesting that this is more important than resolution of the particular problem, even though their apparent reason for the counselling was to find help to resolve the problem.

It means that the *process* does demonstrate effectively the evidence that people need that they are genuinely valued for their contribution.

Resolving issues

It is important to acknowledge explicitly that the process does lead to some form of resolution of issues. For the employee, the different form that resolution takes is important.

Employees have come up with the answer or strategies themselves. This means that they are far more likely to put it (or them) into practice. We all prefer our own solutions, and quite rightly—they tend to be more appropriate to our situation and our abilities than those which others suggest. Reflect on this for a moment, in the light of your own experience, because it is a very important point.

Why we prefer our own solutions

If someone suggests a solution or strategy to us, it will tend to be that person's own view of the issue and the situation. Our reaction to the idea is likely to be one of the following:

- *I had already thought of that*   We really only wanted reassurance that we were on the right lines, and resent a little the inference that we could not think of it for ourselves.

- *Yes, but it won't work*   We had thought of this and maybe tried it out and already dismissed it as not being appropriate to resolve the issue. We feel as if they do not really understand the problem.
- *That won't work*   It is an idea we had not thought of, but when we put the issue against it, we do not think it will solve it.
- *I can't do that*   We can see how it would resolve the issue, but we are not sure it is within our capabilities.
- *That would be OK for you*   We recognize that their suggestion would resolve the issue from their point of view, but we are not convinced that it will help us.
- *Why didn't I think of that!*   It is a good idea, and workable, but we feel a bit stupid, because we did not think of it for ourselves.

Only occasionally will we feel genuinely delighted with someone else's solution. By helping someone to find the solution or strategy that will work for them, the workplace counsellor avoids these potential reactions, which can sabotage the best of ideas.

Personal development

Workplace counselling, when undertaken well, leads to significant personal development for those being counselled. This happens in a variety of ways, and can be consciously enhanced.

Resolving issues

The most obvious development is that people engaging in counselling learn how to resolve issues for themselves. By taking them through a structured process of thinking through, the workplace counsellor is educating them in that process, so they begin to be able to apply it for themselves, without needing the guidance.

Because it is relatively simple, and based on ordinary human best practice with others, they can also begin to use it with others, and themselves become workplace counsellors.

Enhanced self-awareness

Through the process of workplace counselling, employees will become more conscious of their own skills and abilities and more confident in applying them. They will also feel able to ask for help in developing skills and abilities which they perceive as useful to them, and take some responsibility for their own development. There is a significant difference between the way in which someone who is dependent asks for help and the way in which someone who has learnt to take responsibility does so. Through effective workplace counselling, we can help people to become more self-managing without becoming irresponsibly confident.

Awareness of other viewpoints

By having attention given to their own viewpoint, employees unconsciously receive the message that other viewpoints are also to be valued. The workplace counsellor is setting an example of how to treat other people's views. This example will be unconsciously absorbed and they will begin to apply it in their interactions with others. This leads to a general improvement in relationships at work.

Enhanced awareness of the organization Because the workplace counselling is clearly designed to help them to make informed decisions, employees are likely to receive useful information about organizational policies, and about other people's general experience. This enriches their awareness and enables them to contribute more effectively.

Benefits to the employee of workplace counselling

- Feeling valued and listened to.
- Solutions which will work for them.
- Learning how to resolve their own issues.
- Enhanced self-awareness.
- Improved work relationships.
- Feeling more involved in and aware of organizational issues.
- Enhanced empowerment.

Counselling for empowerment

When you add together these potential benefits for the employee, if workplace counselling is used well, you have a package for empowerment.

The process contributes significantly to the practical empowerment of individuals, by educating them into taking responsibility for themselves in an informed way. As important by-products it also provides evidence that the organization means what it says when it talks about 'putting people first', and gives managers a method for giving that evidence and preparing themselves and their employees for a changing role.

Key points

- Workplace counselling benefits managers by:
  — increasing their understanding of individuals;
  — enhancing the respect of their staff;
  — reducing the number of problems they have to deal with over time;
  — allowing them to spend more productive time with staff;
  — helping to educate their staff for empowerment with responsibility;
  — developing their skills for a changing role.
- Workplace counselling benefits employees by:
  — making them feel valued;
  — allowing them to find a resolution to the issue which suits their needs;
  — developing their skills in resolving their own issues;
  — enhancing their self-awareness;

- — enhancing their awareness of other viewpoints;
- — increasing their awareness of the organizational context;
- — developing them towards empowerment.
- Workplace counselling benefits the organization by:
  - — increasing the number of people who are genuinely taking responsibility for themselves and their development;
  - — giving practical evidence that the organization values its people;
  - — preparing staff for changing roles.
- Workplace counselling is an essential part of empowerment.

6 Applications of counselling

I have stated several times that workplace counselling is a particular approach to an interaction with an employee, and it applies to a variety of situations. In this chapter, I will look in more detail at the types of situations where workplace counselling is a useful approach.

The circumstances of the intervention

Firstly, we need to consider the circumstances where counselling may be needed. There are two avenues to the counselling situation, and the difference between them can set up the situation in very different ways.

Counselling requested by the employee

In this circumstance, where the employee makes the first move, it is the counsellor who needs to be ready to handle the request.

The employee will already have thought about the issue and will therefore be somewhat prepared. He or she has also had the courage or confidence to make the request, and so is aware of needing some help.

The workplace counsellor, on the other hand, may not even be aware that there is an issue, and is likely to be preoccupied with other things when the request is made. It is therefore essential that we include something in our training and development for workplace counsellors which will help them to be ready to respond to a request for counselling with appropriate behaviour.

If they are not prepared to deal with such requests, there is a danger that they will put off the employee, or not give adequate attention and value to the request, because of other pressures. If this happens, the employee will lose trust in the workplace counsellor, and there will be more widespread negative consequences of a thoughtless moment.

This does not mean that the workplace counsellors have to drop everything to deal with a request for counselling. That would be unrealistic in the workplace. It does mean that they need to acknowledge the request, and find an appropriate way to deal with it properly.

It is also important that the counsellors can recognize that many requests for counselling will be indirect or subtle. The employee may know that he or she needs help, but not be confident enough to request it directly.

Joyce asked her manager one day if the presentation she had given to the meeting was all right. Her manager was surprised by the question, because she knew that Joyce found it difficult to do presentations, and there was a tacit acceptance that hers would never be as thorough or as clear as other people's.

Fortunately, the manager spotted the indirect request for help and sat down with Joyce, asking her what she would really like to be able to achieve in a presentation. Joyce was ready to look at ways of developing this aspect of her skill, and the manager was ready to help her to find ways of doing this.

In training we need to enhance the awareness of workplace counsellors so that they can recognize the indirect request. Such requests require even more careful handling than the direct request, since the former are indicative of a lack of confidence on the part of the employee, who can be put off even more easily because of this.

Counselling imposed on the employee

The second circumstance where counselling is needed poses a different set of problems for the workplace counsellor. This is when it is clear from an employee's behaviour or performance that counselling is required, but the individual is not coming forward to ask for help. Presently, this may only occur when the behaviour has reached the point of requiring some form of internal disciplinary procedure. With workplace counselling skills, the manager or personnel officer should be able to pick up on it before it has reached this stage.

In order to make the approach to offer help, the workplace counsellor needs to develop his or her skills in setting the tone for the interaction. Most employees, if asked to see their manager, react defensively. They are ready for the worst, rather than expecting something useful or pleasing as a result of the meeting. So the workplace counsellor needs to be able to offset their fears, or deal with an aggressive stance, and quickly make the situation safe and comfortable for the employee.

More than that, counsellors may need to be able to gently raise the awareness of the employee so that a problem is recognized. An employee may not even have realized consciously that their work is being affected, and, even if they do know that they are 'under par', they may not know what the cause is.

The workplace counsellor, then, needs a high level of sensitivity to the effects of responses or actions on the employee at the beginning of a counselling session. Initial handling of the situation can make a significant difference to what happens thereafter.

Having looked at the two ways in which a counselling situation may be identified, we need to run through the variety of types of situation where workplace counselling may be useful.

Resolving problems

The most obvious place for counselling is where someone has a personal problem which is affecting their performance at work. The range of such problems is enormous, and within any team of people at any given time, someone will have some personal problem which is affecting their performance. It is awareness of this that makes many managers wary of even beginning to look at workplace counselling. They either do not want to deal with the flood of possibilities or do not want to be drawn into people's personal lives. It is important, therefore, to distinguish between situations where personal problems require workplace counselling, and where they do not.

Dealing with it themselves

A large proportion of personal problems are dealt with by the person concerned without any need for outside help.

Examples would include:

- Worrying about a child because he or she is ill or taking exams.
- Having had a family row the evening before.
- Feeling ill or miserable.
- Having received bad news that morning.
- Feeling fed up with life in general.
- Falling out with a work colleague.

These types of problems are likely to affect work performance temporarily. However, they generally clear up within a day or two, or even an hour or two. They are the normal ups and downs of a human being living an ordinary life.

All they require is some recognition and allowance for a temporary dip in performance. By allowing people to be a little 'under par' for a while, you give them space to work it through more quickly. You are also indirectly telling them that they are valued as a human being, rather than just a working robot, and that they are important enough to you for you to take account of and allow for the slight vagaries of being human.

The result is usually that they recover quickly and give of their best, because the pace was not forced. I have even known staff ask how they could make up for their lapse by doing something extra, because they wanted to show that they appreciated being given the space.

Sometimes the person concerned will not wait and allow the problem to work through. They may come to the workplace counsellor and ask for help. In this situation, the counsellor may choose simply to give the space—and some sympathy.

Alternatively, if it seems useful, the counsellor may engage in workplace counselling to help the person to find their own best and most effective way of dealing with it. By encouraging the employee to use common sense to help them through a temporary patch, and by putting it into the context of 'normal', the workplace counsellor reduces the likelihood of having to deal with such problems with that person again.

A need for workplace counselling

It is when one of these normal ups and downs of life is *not* clearing that there is a need for workplace counselling. Being fed up for a day is normal, being fed up for a week or more suggests that help is needed to work out how to shift the mood.

Not getting on with a work colleague for a day or two because of a disagreement is normal. Continuing not to get on with people suggests that they need some help in looking at how they relate to others.

Even with issues which may take some time to resolve, such as worrying about their children, or an emotional problem, there is a point at which they should be managing themselves at work, despite the problem. If they are not finding a way of coping with it, then there is a need for workplace counselling.

Beyond workplace counselling

One of the major fears of workplace counsellors is that they may be faced with personal problems which they do not think they can handle. Workplace counselling is similar to dealing with a friend or family member. In that circumstance we are more likely to admit that it is something we cannot deal with, because we do not have the title of counsellor. Similarly, workplace counsellors need to feel that it is all right to say that a person's problems are such that they feel that they cannot help as much as they would like to.

The workplace counsellor is not an expert in counselling. He or she is someone who uses a counselling approach as part of a toolkit in dealing with people.

> An example might be dealing with someone whose spouse has left them. In the first place, the workplace counsellor may help the person to begin to come to terms with their own feelings, and may be able to help the person to find ways of taking hold of life again. However, if the individual has strong anger or grief, the help may be required of a professional counsellor who specializes in relationship problems.

It is important that the workplace counsellor feels able to say that he or she cannot be effective in helping the individual, and refers the person to a more useful source of help.

Diagnosis of the situation In all three areas of dealing with personal problems, the workplace counsellor needs the sensitivity and awareness to be able to select accurately the appropriate approach. In training counsellors, we need to ensure that they are aware of these distinctions, can diagnose accurately and act accordingly.

Although the area of personal problems is the one which first comes to mind when we talk about workplace counselling, it is probably relatively minor in terms of the times workplace counselling will be useful. Far more workplace counselling will be focused on the following types of situation.

Dealing with poor work performance

Traditionally, the problem of people's work not being up to scratch has been dealt with either by telling them they had to improve, or by getting rid of them. Where the employer or manager showed more thought, he or she may have suggested training to the individuals, or at least asked them to explain the cause of the problem.

By using workplace counselling, the manager or personnel officer can arrive at a strategy for dealing with the problem more effectively. Poor work performance falls into three categories:

- Competence at the tasks.
- Relationships with others.
- Coping with change.

Competence at the tasks When people are falling short of the performance required in the tasks they are responsible for, there is a variety of possible reasons for this.

For example, people who turn out the required quality of end product, but take far too long to do so may be under-achieving because:

- They are being over-careful with the work.
- They do not know how to do it more efficiently.
- They feel that the time estimated for the task is too little.
- They prefer that task to others they have to do.
- They think that they will get away with it.
- They are not really motivated by the task.

In this instance, it is vital to check out which is the real reason, because the solution would be different for each one. What is more, the counsellor would need to check carefully, because the employees concerned may give what they see as the most acceptable reason, to diminish the negative reaction, rather than the reason which has most effect on them.

With skilful workplace counselling, you can identify with them the real reason for under-achieving, and the most appropriate way of resolving it, so that the likelihood of a genuine improvement in performance is increased.

Relationships with others
Poor work relationships have a more negative effect on work performance than anything else. When you talk to almost any group of people about their work, the thing that demotivates them will tend to be the behaviour of others, and this covers a wide range of behaviours: bullying, authoritarian, dismissive, condescending, interfering, gossiping, refusing to join in, not contributing, interrupting, being rude, being too familiar, being unfriendly—the list goes on and on.

Whereas you can specify in detail the requirements for effective completion of a task, it is not possible to lay down behavioural specifications in an effective way, although some have attempted to do so. The problem is that appropriate behaviour varies according to the individuals and situation involved. Behaviour is also driven by attitude, and the 'right' behaviour with the 'wrong' attitude does not have the desired effect.

> An example of this that I came across recently concerned a bully. He was told to stop bullying, and was told the specific evidence of bullying, and how he had to behave instead. The comment from a colleague was: 'He's still a nasty piece of work, and I wouldn't trust him as far as I can throw him, but at least he doesn't reduce me to tears in front of other colleagues now.'

What is needed to improve work relationships is to recognize the attitudes or beliefs which cause the symptomatic behaviour, and to identify ways of helping the person concerned to change the attitude or belief, so that they can develop more appropriate behaviour in a genuine way.

With skilful workplace counselling, you could achieve a more useful change in behaviour. By recognizing with the individual that there are beliefs and attitudes which lead to such behaviour—in the case of bullying, often to do with what will make people take notice of them, how you control people, etc.—and helping him to identify how else he could achieve the same effect—that is, be taken notice of, and feel in control—without negative side-effects such as lack of trust, fear, dislike—you could effect a change in behaviour which was more widespread than just a halt to the direct bullying.

It would be a change which he had chosen and was comfortable with, therefore more likely to be put into practice. It would also have been arrived at in a sympathetic way, rather than through a telling-off, so the individual felt empowered rather than further diminished by the interaction.

> A typical comment from the bully who has experienced this counselling approach would be: 'I didn't realize how much what I was doing had a bad effect on others, and on me. I feel more able to handle other people now, and I enjoy my work more.' And colleagues are likely to say: 'He's a changed person.'

Coping with change

This category is a relatively new item on the agenda. It would appear as a category of work-related problems once in a while before the 1980s, but would only be a temporary problem.

Now it is recognized to be a major reason for poor work performance, and one which needs to be continuously revisited, as change in organizations is continuous rather than a one-off occurrence.

It has come as a surprise in many organizations to realize that those who remain in the business after de-layering and re-structuring processes are significantly demoralized by the process, even though they could be seen as the ones who are all right, because they are still there.

The so-called 'survivors' syndrome' leaves people feeling insecure and unsure of their future. Rather than prompting them through fear into improving their performance, it tends to have the opposite effect of making them tense and anxious, and therefore producing a worse performance. It is as important to offer support and help to the survivors as it is to those who lose their positions.

Besides this, there are the changes in roles and responsibilities, the changes in general working practice, and the changes in technology and processes, all of which may make people feel unsure of themselves. This is particularly true for the older employees, as they were not brought up to expect change to be a constant feature of the workplace.

By recognizing the potential negative effects of changing organizational and working practice, the workplace counsellor can use his or her skills to help the individual come to terms with the changes and develop an ability to live with uncertainty. The counsellor can also help people to start to positively thrive on change and see it as a part of normal working practice.

Disciplinary problems

We normally think of disciplinary procedures as being separate from counselling problems. However, as stated earlier, a good manager or personnel officer will pick up the problem before it goes as far as official disciplining and can often help people to mend their ways before it is a matter of procedure.

This benefits the individuals concerned, the manager and the organization, as it avoids a lengthy, demoralizing and essentially negative approach to such problems, as well as giving individuals a chance to reconsider the results of their behaviour before it is too late.

The most common problems leading to disciplinary proceedings are absence, lateness and poor work performance. We have already looked at the area of poor work performance and proposed that it could be picked up and dealt with more effectively through workplace counselling. By using the counselling approach, you are more likely to identify the real root cause of the poor performance, and help individuals to find resolutions which they can work with.

Absence and lateness

Similarly with persistent absence or lateness, it is likely that these are symptoms rather than causes. In other words, the behaviour tells you something is wrong, but stopping the behaviour will not necessarily cure the wrong. By using workplace counselling skills, you can find out with individuals the underlying cause and help them to find a way of dealing with it, which is much more effective than either punishing absence or lateness, or even rewarding attendance and punctuality.

It is also noticeable that when you look to find the causes, they are usually linked in to the previous two categories of issues: personal problems or poor work performance.

Square pegs in round holes

When the behaviour of an individual has reached the point of being potentially a reason for disciplinary procedures, despite the attempts of the manager or personnel officer to get the person to recognize the potential negative results of such behaviour, and to find ways of improving, then it may be time to consider whether they are in fact in the right job.

No one will continue to risk their job if they can do something about it, unless they really cannot come to terms with the job itself. Such behaviour is unlikely to be deliberate—it is more likely to be an unconscious cry for help.

With workplace counselling, you can help the person to re-evaluate their position, and recognize that they would be more likely to succeed if they were to look for a post which suited their skills and qualities better. This is far more useful to both the individual and the organization than the eventual pushing out of someone through disciplinary proceedings. It gives both sides the opportunity to deal with the situation constructively.

> Bill had worked on the assembly line for 20 years. He knew how to do the job, yet had recently fallen into a somewhat cavalier approach to his work. He was absent with 'flu', his work was not always up to scratch, and he frequently fell out with colleagues. When reviewing his performance with him, his manager decided to try to find out what was going on behind this behaviour. She asked Bill to talk about work, and discovered that he had always wanted to be a gardener, but felt that he could not keep his family by doing that. He did landscaping in his spare time, and had quite a reputation for his work. His love for this made him feel frustrated on the line. He also felt that he was reaching an age where he would never be able to fulfil his dream, because he would lose his fitness.

Between them, they established that his financial burden was less now that his children were grown, and his mortgage was paid. From there, they went on to discuss the possibility of him making a business out of his gardening.

By supporting the individuals in their search for a more appropriate alternative, the manager or personnel officer not only makes their own role in the process a more comfortable one—few people like being the instigator of disciplinary procedure—they also demonstrate to staff that individuals are valued.

Exit counselling

This leads on to another area where workplace counselling skills are invaluable. Their use when someone is leaving the work situation can make a significant difference. There are two distinct types of situation where someone is leaving: one is where the individual has chosen to leave for positive reasons, for example, to go to a better job; and the other is where the individual has to leave, for example, through redundancy. It is not quite as clear-cut as this: someone who is retiring may be pleased to be going, or wish that they did not have to go. The distinction is in how the person concerned feels about it.

Where the move is seen as detrimental to the individual

Where the person does not feel that there are gains to be made by leaving, there is sometimes a process already in place to give help and support in dealing with it. For example, many organizations now have specialized redundancy or outplacement counselling services. These services can give the in-depth support which is needed, but these individuals will still want and gain from some first-line support from managers. It makes a significant difference to feeling valued if the manager offers their support through workplace counselling as well. After all, this is the person with whom they have been working, and so the reaction of this person to their situation carries more weight than that of an outsider.

Managers are often relieved not to have to deal with the problem, because they find it difficult to handle the person's reactions, whether that be aggression or upset. Yet whatever the behaviour, most people are feeling unwanted and uncared for when they are displaced, and the manager's concern and care in this situation can help considerably.

With workplace counselling skills the manager can help people to feel that they have been valuable, and to begin to consider what they will do next in a more positive way.

This is even more important where the person's situation is not automatically referred for outside support. For example, there may be someone who is leaving because their partner has got a better job in another part of the country. This person will gain a lot from workplace counselling to help them come to terms with the move, rather than avoidance of the subject because everyone feels sympathy.

Where the move is seen as positive When someone is leaving a job by choice, there tends to be an assumption that there is no need to offer workplace counselling.

Yet the added value of offering that opportunity is significant for the individual concerned. As someone said to me: 'I believed that the company thought highly of me, but when I got a new job, they just seemed to wash their hands of me, and it really undermined my confidence.'

By spending time with the individual giving explicit value to what they had achieved in their work, and encouraging the individual to look at how they could use their strengths in the new job, a manager would significantly change this feeling.

Why bother? When someone is leaving, it may not seem worth devoting time and energy to workplace counselling. After all, you will not benefit directly from any positive difference it makes to them.

However, there are significant less obvious benefits.

Firstly, there is a benefit to the manager or personnel officer. Most will say that they feel uncomfortable about how they handle someone who is leaving, and this will turn that around.

Secondly, other staff notice how people are treated, and it affects their perception of the value given to people in the organization. If the manager gives time and attention to people who are leaving, where there is no obvious selfish reason for it, this sends out an important message about the way the organization values people in general.

So far we have looked primarily at areas for workplace counselling which have a problem orientation. But counselling is not only useful in problem situations, as is illustrated by the example of someone who is leaving for a better alternative.

As managers apply workplace counselling more and more, they should find that the number of problems diminishes and they can put their primary attention on developmental rather than remedial counselling.

Developmental counselling

The workplace counselling approach is ideally suited to enabling individuals to take more and more responsibility for their own development. In the changing world of organizations the continuous development of individual skills and qualities is essential to the success of the organization, and so this outcome becomes more and more desirable.

There are probably already systems in place, which are intended to enable this form of performance development. What workplace counselling offers is the appropriate approach to applying these systems, in order to produce the desired effect.

Performance management systems

Appraisals

Often managers regard appraisals as a necessary evil rather than an added value activity. It is seen as an additional burden of responsibility and makes little difference to the actual performance of staff. This has led to some organizations calling the process something different, such as personal development programmes, to try to get away from that image.

But when the counselling approach is used, employees take on more responsibility for their own part in the appraisals, and it can be used to genuinely identify and create opportunities for development which they will take up and use.

Ongoing monitoring

Where there is a well-developed performance management system, there will be other opportunities to apply the counselling approach to encourage development, through feedback sessions, team reviews, personal development reviews, etc. Even if these do not exist as a formal system, the manager can use informal situations to apply counselling skills in a developmental way.

For example, as he or she walks about, and talks to people about their work in hand, the manager can ask how people feel that they are progressing in their work. By setting the questions in the context of a workplace counselling approach, the manager will be continuously encouraging the staff to consider their own development.

Through the informal counselling approach, Frank discovered that
his administrative assistant would like to be able to train others in
business administration one day. This led to them taking on a
trainee to work with the administrative assistant, to see how she
got on in training an individual. When this worked well, it led to
the administrative assistant asking how she could develop her
skills further. She is now working full time as a recognized trainer
in office skills.

Using developmental counselling

If the organization wants to succeed in a rapidly changing world, then
this form of counselling is vital. It encourages the habit in people of
constantly looking for ways to improve their performance—a
prerequisite for a successful organization.

Managers know that they need to encourage this approach to work in
their staff—what they do not know, often, is how to. Workplace
counselling can give them the key.

I have identified the many ways in which this approach can be useful to
managers and personnel officers. If they learn to develop their skills in
counselling for empowerment, they will find that they have to spend
less of their time dealing with crises and major problems, because their
staff will take on more and more responsibility for their own
performance.

Through the counselling approach, they will enable their staff to know
how to be empowered, personally and professionally, to solve
problems and make decisions, because they will be offering them a
process they can apply for themselves. This will free up the manager or
personnel officer to concentrate on building confidence and
encouraging development. As these take hold, the manager becomes
the resource and encourager and can concentrate on giving value to the
individuals in their team. This is an upward spiral that every
organization must aspire to, and is within the realms of possibility.

Key points

- Counselling skills may be needed as a response to a request from
staff or as a proactive intervention from the manager or personnel
officer. They need to be prepared for both types of application.
- Workplace counselling can be useful in the following circumstances:
  — Resolving problems, either by offering reassurance and support
  or by helping the person to work through to a resolution, or by
  referring the person on to an appropriate specialist.
  — Dealing with poor work performance. This may be competence

at the task, or in work relationships, and may be caused by an inability to cope with change.

— Disciplinary problems, to pick them up and resolve them before they reach the stage of formal proceedings. This may include recognizing that the problem is one of appropriate job, and need for review of career.

— Exit counselling, with those who are pleased to leave as well as those who regret losing their position.

— Developmental counselling, through formal and informal means, to inculcate the habit of continuous improvement.

- The application of the workplace counselling approach requires sensitivity and a willingness to find out rather than assume on the part of the manager or personnel officer.
- The need for the remedial workplace counselling will diminish over time and allow more opportunity for developmental counselling.
- By using the approach in this wide range of situations, the manager or personnel officer creates an environment which is empowering and demonstrates that people are valued.

PART THREE

Needs of workplace counsellors

In Part 3 we begin to look in detail at the qualities and skills which we intend to develop in workplace counsellors. Where appropriate, there are descriptions of how you might enable the development suggested to give you extra resource material to call on when you come to plan a development programme. This part gives a thorough description of the potential elements of a development programme for workplace counsellors.

7 Self-management

In order to be effective in workplace counselling, people who are going to develop their skills in enabling others need to start by developing their skills in managing themselves.

The attitude and behaviour of the counsellor have a significant effect on the usefulness of the counselling, and this needs to be made explicit.

How you are affects what happens

Everyone will recognize that the attitude of those giving counselling affects the effectiveness of the counselling, but somehow we manage to convince ourselves that it does not apply to us! Most of us can think of examples, whether it be people who try too hard to help, and make us feel as if they are interfering, or people who doubt their own ability to be helpful who infect us with their doubt, or people who are doing it because they should, not because they genuinely want to.

It is important to point out that they probably do not realize that their underlying attitudes are affecting the usefulness of their skills. This effect is at an unconscious level, and although we all get a sense of it from others, we do not usually recognize it in ourselves.

We need to make people more aware of the effect of their own state on the usefulness of their counselling, by getting them to realize that they react to others at an unconscious level and that it has an effect on their state or attitude. And then we need to give them strategies which will help them to manage their own state more effectively.

Managing your state

Most people think that their state or mood 'happens', that they have no control over it, but are victims of circumstance. Before you can offer these strategies, you need to remind people that they can take control, and already *do* know how to change their state.

A good example of this is when someone is tired after a hard day's work, and only feels like slumping in front of the television. Yet if a friend phones, and suggests a social evening, many people make an almost instant recovery! They may have a shower and get changed, and by the time they are leaving, they feel ready for an evening's fun.

This illustrates several of the factors which help us to change our state:

1 The reason for changing state is attractive—it is worth making the effort, in our view.
2 We know it is possible—we have done the same thing before.
3 Changing our physical state helps to change our mental state.

Telling ourselves that it will be fun, that is, changing the messages in our head, helps to overcome our original physical state of tiredness.

Most people will also have numerous examples of changing from a positive to a negative state, such as: 'I feel fed up as soon as someone mentions the team meeting.' It is less useful to explore these examples, although it is important to acknowledge that they still demonstrate the ability to change state instantly!

A reason for changing state
The first factor to consider when looking at ways to manage yourself is what reasons you have for bothering to do so. We are basically fairly selfish creatures, and unless we can identify some benefit to ourselves for making the difference, we are unlikely to do it.

In the example above, if the person phoning was someone you did not particularly like, or if the last time you went out was boring, or if they were suggesting a disco and you do not like dancing, you would have probably stayed with being exhausted!

The benefits we respond to differ significantly as well. You cannot assume, just because you think it is worth doing, because you believe it will make you feel good, that anyone else will see it in the same light. One man's meat is another man's poison.

If the workplace counsellors are to be motivated to change their state, they need to identify the benefits for themselves which actually work for them. We cannot tell them that they should be motivated, no matter how convincing the reasons are for us.

Throughout Part 1, I identified some of the issues which the changes in organizational practice have raised, and proposed that workplace counselling could contribute to overcoming these issues. This sort of information can give some people the motivation they need.

In Chapter 5, I identified some of the specific positive effects which may accrue to managers as well as staff through the skilful use of workplace counselling. These may give you the starting point for people to identify the benefits which they perceive as worth while.

It is still important to ensure that everyone finds the ones which work for them personally, and to allow for the full range of potential motivators:

- One person will be more motivated by the idea of being seen as helpful to others.
- Another will be more motivated by the possibility of making their working life easier.
- A third will be more motivated by the opportunity to enhance their employability.

Most people will need a mixture of benefits, to make it worth their while to take the process to the next step.

The source of our mood or attitude

When you track back to identify the source of our approach to a situation, it will usually depend on our beliefs, values and expectations. To illustrate this, just reflect on any recent situation you were involved in, and ask yourself, 'Why did I approach it/react to it in that way?' The answer is likely to begin with: 'because I thought that ...' and then give a list of the assumptions you made about the situation.

We all do make assumptions about any situation we are going into, to help us decide how to approach the situation, and these assumptions are based on our beliefs and values. For example, if I assume a particular situation will be hard for me to handle, that assumption may be because I lack belief in my own abilities and skills, or because I believe that the particular group will be hostile or resistant in some way to my ideas. If it is important to me to get my message across—my values—I may make an extra effort to overcome the effect of those beliefs.

The beliefs and values which drive our behaviour may be quite unconscious. We may think that we are dealing with objective facts. Yet this is clearly not the case. Different people approach the same situation with different attitudes and have a different result or effect.

> Philip was dreading his staff appraisal. He 'knew' he did not come across well, and the boss was new and did not know him. On the other hand, Jane was looking forward to her appraisal. The boss was new, and that gave her a chance to make a new impression, without previous assumptions. They both approached the same objective situation quite differently.

What we do is notice evidence which supports the beliefs or values we take into the situation, and use that as proof we were right.

> Philip came out of the appraisal feeling that he had not made a good impression. The boss seemed to agree with him that he needed to undertake a list of developments, so obviously did not rate him highly.
>
> Jane came out feeling pleased. The boss had obviously liked and agreed with her action plan for her own development.

Changing beliefs to change state

When we become aware that this is the process that creates our state, the way we approach things, then we can do something about it.

We can begin to choose what assumptions we will make, and what beliefs and values we will find evidence for.

Most of us have a wide range of beliefs and values, many of which can be seen as contradictory. For example, we may believe in human potential, yet have criteria which lead us to assume that some people are bound to be stupid. This is normal, and few of us are totally consistent in our values and beliefs—it is part of that mixture of qualities called a human being. Rather than trying to make ourselves consistent, we can exploit the potential of having a wide repertoire of beliefs and values, so that it becomes useful to us.

Beliefs about self

By asking managers and personnel officers which are the beliefs they hold about themselves which would be *useful* to take into a counselling situation, you focus their attention on those which will elicit in them the right state.

They are likely to come up with statements like:

- 'I believe I'm fair.'
- 'I believe I get on well with other people.'
- 'I believe I listen carefully.'

They may also want to list the beliefs about themselves which will give them a negative state: 'I'm impatient', 'I'm judgemental', etc. When they do so, I would suggest that you just ask them if it would be useful for them to focus on this belief in the counselling situation.

Once they have selected the beliefs about themselves which would be useful, it is important to reinforce those beliefs. This can be done by asking them to talk about times when they demonstrated that quality, and to remember situations where they were being like that. This helps to remind them consciously of the evidence they already have to support the belief. As they do this, you can ask them to notice how it makes them feel, so they recognize that the beliefs we focus on affect our attitude and behaviour. In my experience, people talking about times when they have been fair, patient, good at relating to others, etc., actually behave according to those principles within the discussion.

They then need a reminder to bring those beliefs to the fore when they are about to engage in workplace counselling. Since we unconsciously set ourselves up for a situation by the assumptions we make, we can equally decide consciously to set ourselves up in a way which is more useful. By devising a short statement to say to themselves before counselling, they can counteract the unconscious assumptions. Such a statement might be:

'I want to help this person. I will be able to handle the situation, and I can be fair and tolerant. I will be sensitive to their needs, and listen carefully.'

Beliefs about others   In the same way, we can consider the beliefs held about other people, and select those which are most useful. Usually we select according to what we have noticed or been told.

> I remember, as a very young teacher in a secondary modern school, being given two different pieces of advice about the students. The head said, 'These children are stupid, because they failed the entrance examination, so don't expect them to learn much, just keep them quiet.' An older teacher said, 'If you treat these children as stupid, they will be naughty and disruptive, so assume they want to learn, and they will respond to you.' I chose to take the latter's advice, and discovered that the students were delightful and eager learners!

If I had not been given the contradictory messages, and thereby forced to think about what I would find more useful, I may have ended up just trying to keep my students quiet—an arduous and boring task.

By stopping to consider what our useful beliefs about others are, we can select those which will help us to approach both the situation and the person more positively. To do this, you go through the same process as for beliefs about ourselves:

1 Identify useful beliefs about others in counselling. You can expect such statements as: 'people can solve their own problems'; 'people want to improve their situation or skills'; 'no one wants to be a victim'.
2 Get the trainee counsellors to talk about evidence they have to support these beliefs. Remind them that they are 'people' too, so they can use themselves as well as others as examples.
3 Ask them to notice how this discussion affects their attitude to others while they are talking.

4　Ask them to add to the statement they will make to themselves before engaging in counselling. It might be something like:

This person wants to and is able to resolve their own issue with a little help. Any reluctance will be because they're not used to the approach, not because they don't want it.

Knowing how to be more resourceful

The techniques for identifying useful beliefs focus attention on the positive benefits and potential positive effects of workplace counselling. They enable the 'spirit to be willing', but we still have to deal with the 'flesh being weak'.

Successful workplace counselling requires that the counsellors are feeling resourceful in the first place. It is a demanding approach, and needs a constructive state of mind and a reasonable level of positive energy. Within the workplace context there are many demands on the energy of the workplace counsellors which can drain them, and leave them with an inappropriate state of mind for counselling. It is vital therefore to remind them that there are techniques which can be used in preparation for the session to enhance their resourcefulness. They do not take long, so are practicable within the workplace, yet they can significantly help the successful use of the approach.

Reviving energy

Everyone needs to revive their energy, although we are often lax in doing so! By stopping and taking the space to make yourself feel re-energized, you can often achieve twice as much as you do by keeping going with the tasks in front of you without recharging the batteries. This is common sense, but that does not mean that people automatically do it.

How individuals raise their energy will vary, so they have to make their own choices, but it is useful to remind them of commonly used strategies, and encourage them to consider their own most useful ones for the work context.

Physical activity

Many people find a short walk will liven them up, especially if it includes a breath of fresh air. The physical movement helps to shift both their physical and mental state, and will quickly relieve the symptoms of stress and fatigue. This effect is enhanced if they also breathe deeply while doing it.

In the work context, it may be possible to take a walk around the outside of the building. If not, stand up and walk down the corridor. Even just going to make or fetch a drink, or rinse your face, should release the physical tensions and allow the energy to flow again.

Sensory attention

Many people find that they liven up if they come out of their heads for a few minutes and focus on their senses. Something that you like the sound of, the taste of, the smell of, or the feel of, can lift flagging energy levels.

In the workplace context, such sensory pleasures may not be abundant, but they can easily be consciously arranged. People can have photos, cartoons, or plants that they like the look of; they can maybe listen to the birdsong outside, or even sing a favourite song to themselves; they can bring a favourite taste with them—an apple, a sweet, a drink of something; they can go to the washroom and splash on a bit of scent or aftershave, or smell the plants they have; they may have an executive toy, or pebbles, or a juggling ball that they like to play with to appeal to the sense of touch.

Most people can find something of this ilk on which to focus their attention for a few moments. What matters is that it makes them smile or feel good for those moments. It is therefore idiosyncratic—what makes one person feel good may not appeal to another.

Relaxation For some people, stopping for a few moments and relaxing, physically and mentally, will refresh them. It is worth offering some specific techniques for doing this within the work context. You may have your own favourite methods, and can develop lots more, but I will give one example.

Find a quiet corner where you can take a couple of minutes on your own without disturbance. (If you don't have one, a toilet cubicle works fine!)

Concentrate on making your feet as tense as possible, and then relax them.

Now move to your legs and tense all the muscles and then relax them.

Move to your stomach. Hold it in tightly, then relax.

Now do the same with your buttocks.

Pull your shoulders as far back as they will go, and then relax.

Now pull your shoulders forward, tightening your chest and relax.

Now hunch your shoulders up, and then relax them down.

Tighten the muscles in your arms, and then relax.

Clench your fists, then relax.

Rotate your head in a clockwise direction: back as far as you can, then over to one side, then as close to your chest as you can, then to the other side.

Repeat in the opposite direction.

Finally screw up all your facial muscles and then relax them.

Finish by taking three deep breaths. Do this by expelling all the air you can from your lungs, and then allowing the in-breath to happen on its own.

If you add to this a breathing pattern, you enhance the physical and mental relaxation, as it becomes almost a meditation. Breathe in with tension and out with relaxation, and count the breaths. (There are only 12, which illustrates that it does not take long.)

I find that people often have their own methods—stretching, being like a rag doll, breathing exercises, etc.—but do not think to use them at work. Whatever they like doing will work best for them.

Imagination

If there is no available other way to refresh themselves, people can always use their imagination. By just closing our eyes and thinking about things which revive us, we can often achieve almost as good an effect as when we are actually doing the things for real.

You could also suggest that they remember times when they have felt energized, and then imagine themselves going into the counselling situation in that state.

A combination package

It is often possible to combine these different ways of refreshing ourselves. Obviously, the more we have, the more refreshed we will feel. For example, a short walk could include all of them: physical activity; sensory attention to the outside world; relaxation of the mind by attention on other things; relaxation of the body by walking slowly and breathing deeply; and imaginary refreshment through thinking of times when we were energized.

After setting up a foundation of feeling energized, it is then important to prepare the mind-set for the particular activity.

Clearing the mind

Most of the time we have other things on our mind: what we have just been doing; what we are going to do after the next activity; what is important to us for that day; what is bothering us for that day; or maybe just that we need to get to the bank before it closes! Carrying this muddle of thoughts in our heads is actually distracting all of the time. However, when someone is about to engage in workplace counselling, it is essential that they are able to put aside other thoughts and have a clear mind for the task in hand.

Again, there is a variety of strategies someone can use. It is worth having at least one to suggest, while accepting that individuals may use different ones.

One obvious strategy is just to note down the various things you are thinking about, so that you do not have to keep them in your head. You can then refer back to the piece of paper after the counselling session and pick up where you left off.

Setting your expectations

Before we engage in any activity, we always set ourselves up for it in some way, by telling ourselves about it. We do this so automatically that we often do not realize what we have done.

Examples might be:

- 'This meeting will be boring.'
- 'I want to get this over and done with.'
- 'I bet so-and-so will be awkward.'
- 'I'm really looking forward to this.'
- 'Ms Smith is always interesting to talk with.'
- 'I want to do this well.'

Having cleared your mind, it helps consciously to tell yourself what your expectation is in the counselling situation. I have already suggested, under the section on beliefs, that people construct a brief statement for themselves. They may wish to add to that a couple more sentences which capture the essence of what the session will ideally be like:

- 'This will be constructive and interesting.'
- 'I want to ensure that it is useful for both of us.'

You can get people to devise a range of such useful statements, from which they can select the ones that appeal to them most individually.

Being ready to pay attention to others

The final area of self-management to consider is the readiness to be sensitive to and pay attention to others. In order to do this, we need to ensure that the environment and our physical state are conducive to attending to others.

The environment

It is obvious that in a counselling situation we need to clear the environment of distractions. Yet in the workplace it is sometimes more difficult to achieve, and requires some thought.

- Is there a private space they can take someone to?
- Can they have their phone calls re-directed?
- Can they shut out interruptions from others?
- If they are stopped by someone in a busy, noisy environment, can they move into a different environment?
- If nowhere else is possible, could they walk outside with the person, or go to a café for the session?

Physical state

To offer good attention to someone else, we need to be comfortable in ourselves, so that we are not distracted by our own discomfort. It is important to have been to the lavatory, had a drink or something to eat, and completed any other actions which might otherwise distract you during the session. It is then important to make sure that you are physically comfortable, whether sitting, standing or walking. If you ask people to identify what makes them feel comfortable, you remind them that until they are comfortable, they will not be able to pay attention to the other person, or put them at ease.

So far, I have concentrated on the preparation a person needs to be successful in workplace counselling. You will notice that this is all about getting into the right frame of mind to adopt a useful approach.

Normally, when we talk about preparation, we concentrate on the preparation of material, agendas, plans, etc. In workplace counselling, it is the preparation of the right state which will make the most difference.

Self-management within the counselling process

If someone has set themselves up appropriately for the counselling situation, then self-management within the process will tend to be automatically available. There are a few circumstances where people may lose the appropriate mind-set which they have created, and it is worth drawing attention to these, and identifying ways of dealing with them.

Agreeing with the sentiment

When we sympathize strongly with the person, it can take us out of the counselling role, and stop us from being effective in helping the person to resolve the issue.

There are two ways this can happen. The first is where we identify strongly with the issue and relate to it on a personal level. For example, a member of staff may voice feelings of insecurity in their job to a manager who has the same feeling about his or her own job. It is easy in this situation to get drawn into agreeing with the complainant, and expressing your own fears and anxieties. The person may feel slightly better to know that they are not alone in having this feeling, but they are unlikely to feel empowered to do something about it if the manager cannot see a way out!

The second is where someone is very upset about something. This may be a work situation or something personal like a bereavement. Getting caught up in the upset and being as sad and upset as they are may show great empathy, but it is not useful in helping the person to move from that state.

Sympathetic detachment

It is important to be able to sympathize with the feelings while staying out of the state of mind. To help people to do this, you can suggest to them that they ask themselves: 'What would be more useful to help this person to be empowered to deal with this?'

If they find themselves getting caught into the other person's state of mind, suggest that they physically move. This usually helps us to regain our detachment.

No way out

Linked to the situation above, is the one where the counsellors cannot themselves see a potential for resolving the issue. This often happens when we over-identify with the person and their present state of mind.

It is important that counsellors remind themselves of their intention in engaging in the session: to help the person to find their own way of dealing effectively with the situation. Agreeing that it is impossible is not useful, so they need a different approach.

Making it possible To bring themselves back to a constructive frame of mind, counsellors may again choose to physically move themselves, and then remind themselves of the following:

1 If it really were impossible in the person's mind to find a way through, they would not have bothered to consult with you. They just have not found it alone.
2 The issue may be too big to resolve in one step, but you may be able to help them find some ways of bringing it down to size by taking control of things they can affect. By taking small steps to reduce the size of the issue, the person may find the momentum to tackle the larger part.
3 Even if it really is impossible to resolve the issue, it is always possible to modify our reaction to it. By looking at how they can reduce its negative effect, we can help the person to be more empowered.

An obvious way out The opposite situation to the one above is equally likely to pull the workplace counsellor out of the appropriate frame of mind for offering effective counselling. This is where the manager or personnel officer is convinced that they know the answer. This is particularly likely where they have asked the member of staff to come for a session because they have identified a problem, rather than the problem being identified by the member of staff.

An example might be where a member of staff says that he or she wants to develop personal skills, to enhance chances of promotion. If the manager has noticed that the person's spelling is poor, and that they do not like writing things down, the manager may be convinced that the person should take a literacy course.

In this situation, the counsellor is very likely to try to lead the person to the 'right answer', rather than encourage the person to find his or her own answer. What is more, the counsellor is likely to become quite frustrated if the person insists on going in a different direction.

It is important to remind counsellors that what is obviously the right answer from our point of view may not be the right answer for the person concerned. If you ask them to illustrate this point by identifying times when people have given them the 'right answer' and it did not really work for them, you will make them aware of how ineffective this approach is.

Even when the person's answer does coincide with what the counsellor thinks, it is vital to enable them to reach that conclusion in their own way. By doing so, the person 'owns' the solution fully, and is also learning about the process of finding answers, which is as much a part of the counselling as is the solution itself.

When counsellors find themselves trying to get the person to 'guess the right answer' they need to remember these points. When they can see an obvious way out, it is also helpful to say to themselves: 'I wonder if they will reach the same conclusion?' This makes it an interesting journey of discovery, rather than a frustrating attempt to reach the answer.

Clashes of values

The final type of situation where the counsellor may find it difficult to keep the appropriate state of mind is where the individual is expressing beliefs or values which clash with ones which the counsellor holds dear. When this happens, it is hard for the counsellor to stop from judging the individual, and wanting to argue the case.

Rather than judging that he or she is wrong, the counsellor needs to stop and ask: 'Is this useful for the person concerned?' By doing so, the counsellor considers it from the point of view of the staff member, rather than from their own stance.

For example, someone may say that another work colleague is uncooperative, whom you believe to be cooperative and helpful. However much you disagree, you will not help the individual to resolve the issues by saying that they are wrong. You may, however, discover that they have found it useful to blame this person, and therefore see no way out. You could then encourage them to recognize that this usefulness is limited, as it leaves the individual disempowered, and another belief could give them more control of the situation.

On the other hand, if someone were to demonstrate a belief which clashes with very deeply held personal beliefs of the counsellor, it may not be possible to detach from the judgement. An example might be someone who is considering abortion with a counsellor who strongly feels that abortion is wrong. In this instance, I would advise the counsellor to refer that person to someone else.

Techniques to regain state

Whenever workplace counsellors find themselves losing their ability to be objective and useful to the person being counselled, they need to metaphorically step back. In the breath-space or two they then take they can just remind themselves of their purpose in being counsellors— to enable the person to come to a resolution of an issue which will work for them.

None of us approach a situation with complete neutrality. We can put our tendencies to jump to assumptions and judgements on hold by having as priority our desire to be helpful to others. However, some of our personal beliefs and values will over-ride this desire, and that needs to be acknowledged.

Conclusion   Self-management is an essential skill for workplace counsellors. Their state is crucial to the success of the counselling session, and they need to be aware of methods to manage their own state, to help them maintain the appropriate approach.

Is there time?   Although it takes a while to go through these different techniques for self-management, it actually takes little time to put them into place consciously, and their value is significant for both the counsellor and the person being counselled.

Even when the workplace counsellor has been stopped and asked for on-the-spot help, he or she can take the five or ten minutes required for the preparation techniques. I have yet to come across someone who does not want to allow me that time for preparing myself to be able to give them my full attention. People respect you for showing that you want to do it properly rather than half-heartedly.

Similarly, with the session, it takes a breath-space or two to pull yourself back and regain a useful state. Most people will not notice you doing it, although they will benefit from the effect.

Key points
- Self-management provides the basis for an effective counselling approach. Techniques for self-management can be developed and consciously applied, both in the preparation for counselling and in the actual counselling situation.
- It benefits both the counsellor and the person being counselled if the counsellor begins by getting themselves in the appropriate frame of mind.
- Counsellors may need to look at their beliefs about their own capabilities as counsellors, and about how others are likely to react. A simple statement to themselves can help with this, where they have chosen to re-state useful beliefs in the situation.
- Counsellors need techniques for enabling themselves to feel more resourceful. These may include ways of reviving energy, physical activity, relaxation, paying attention through the senses, using their imagination, or a combination of these techniques.
- Counsellors need a method for clearing their mind, so that they come to the situation without extraneous 'baggage' distracting them.
- Into the cleared mind, they need to put a conscious, positive intention for the session.
- Finally they need to ensure that the environment and their physical state are conducive to paying attention to the person concerned. Within the counselling process, counsellors may lose the appropriate frame of mind if:
  — they agree with the sentiments of the person;
  — they empathize too much with the person's negative feelings;

    — they cannot see any resolution themselves;
    — they see an obvious answer for the person;
    — there is a serious clash of values or beliefs in what the person is expressing.

- Counsellors need to recognize that they are losing state and move physically, to give themselves time to find a way to regain a useful frame of mind.
- The reminder to themselves that their intention is to help this person to find an effective way of dealing with the situation can help them to regain state.

8 Confidence and parameters

In the last chapter we looked at ways of helping managers and personnel officers to enhance their skills in self-management. When people feel more in control of their own state of mind and reactions, they also feel more confident in dealing with other people, because they know how to prepare themselves for the interaction.

In this chapter we will explore ways of further enhancing their confidence in taking on the role of workplace counsellor. By increasing their awareness of the qualities and skills required to use this approach well, and giving them an opportunity to try out using their skills in the safer environment of a training session where there is support and help available, we can boost their confidence in approaching real workplace counselling situations.

Doubt in your own ability to perform well is the biggest obstacle to success in developing into an effective workplace counsellor. While we do not want to give people a false confidence, we do need to give them opportunities to discover their own potential. The approach to building confidence that I propose here balances realism and empowerment, to give people a genuine confidence.

What are the skills and qualities of workplace counselling?

The first step to building confidence in being a workplace counsellor is to identify what it requires of the individual. By defining the skills and qualities required, we lay down explicitly the criteria of a good workplace counsellor. I have already given a version in Chapter 4. However, I would take a slightly different approach with a group in training.

By asking them to identify the skills and qualities for themselves, we increase the usefulness of the activity. In my experience of doing this, groups come up with very similar checklists, and variations tend to be in ways of expressing things.

Eliciting the checklist

I usually begin by giving a definition of the workplace counsellor as distinct from the professional counsellor. This is in general terms, such as: 'They enable us to sort out our own solutions. They are rather like a good friend. Their intention is to help us to work out how to deal with our own issues, so that we can perform more effectively.'

I will then give a couple of personal examples of what I consider to be effective workplace counselling, which I have experienced. Of these examples, one will be set in the workplace, but one will be outside it, for example a friend, or my doctor. This is important because for many people the best examples they have personally experienced do not come from the work context. By giving examples, I am both clarifying the definition, and beginning to get people thinking of their own examples.

I then ask them to talk in small groups about their own experience of being counselled effectively. I suggest they comment on what the 'counsellor' was like, their approach, what made it feel useful. After some discussion, they are ready to record their own version of what are the skills and qualities of an excellent workplace counsellor. A typical checklist produced in this way is given in Appendix A.

The benefits of the approach

- People become much clearer about the distinction between the workplace and the professional counsellor.
- They are also beginning to identify potential role models who could be useful in helping them develop their own skills.
- By talking about examples from their own experience, they are beginning to consider effective counselling from the perspective of the person being counselled as well.
- They also adjust and fine-tune their views of what is really effective as they listen to each other.

The resultant checklist is of a high standard and what is more, they 'own' it rather than having a theoretical version imposed on them.

Using the checklist

This checklist gives a useful starting point for exploring how managers and personnel officers might develop these skills and qualities. The first point I make is that our tendency is to compare ourselves to the checklist and give ourselves a 'fail'. At the same time, we can look at the list and recognize that we *have* demonstrated most of those qualities and skills at some point in our lives in some way. There will be some which we are actually good at, and others that we rarely use, and yet others which we are not confident in. This provides the basis for a self-assessment against the checklist, and helps people to recognize their own starting point for development.

I ask them to state out loud one or two of the items off the checklist which they feel they are good at, and one or two that they would like to be better at.

This encourages them to begin by recognizing strengths they can build on, and to re-define areas of weakness as areas for development. There are usually variations in what people select, and by giving them all equal validity as strengths to build on, or areas to develop, we remind people that there is no set pattern to how we develop the skills and qualities. I also propose that when we explore an area they feel that they are already good at, they can contribute more, and when we explore an area they want to develop, they can help motivate the rest of us to explore it thoroughly by taking an active learning role.

Throughout the rest of the training, this checklist provides a referral point, giving a rationale for why we are examining a particular aspect of development. For example, when covering material on self-management, I may refer to the checklist to explain why I am doing it: 'There are several things on the list which are about being in the right state of mind. Here are some ways in which we can consciously create that state of mind.' Or I may refer back to the list after a session on self-management, and say: 'These techniques will be useful if you want to develop these skills and qualities . . . .'

The checklist provides a useful starting point for building confidence that being an excellent workplace counsellor is possible for them.

It is then important to emphasize the fact that the focus on preparation is because feeling ready for the interaction automatically gives more confidence that being an excellent workplace counsellor is possible for them.

We have already looked in detail at the self-management aspects of preparation. Now we will pay some attention to ways of making sure that the person to be counselled is as ready as possible to gain from the interaction.

The following are some main points to consider on how to set the right tone for individuals to benefit most. Knowing that they can manage their own state, and make some simple moves that will help the person to be counselled to be ready, will start them off on the process of workplace counselling with more confidence.

Setting the right tone

The previous chapter was largely about setting yourself up in the right way to take a useful approach to the interaction. This leads on to making sure that you have the right tone for the person being counselled. Obviously, if it makes a difference to your effectiveness to be in the right state, the state the person is in will also affect the process. Although we cannot predict exactly how he or she will be feeling, we can safely predict a few themes and be prepared to deal with those.

Making them feel safe

Most people who have asked for or have been asked to come for a counselling session will be a little anxious. This feeling is likely to be stronger if they are dealing with a personal problem or a serious work-related problem. This anxiety will show clearly in some people. In others it may not be so obvious—in fact they may appear blasé or even aggressive rather than anxious.

None the less, it is worth while for the workplace counsellor to give them some reassurance that the situation will be a safe one for them to be honest in. There are three ways in which he or she can do this.

The environment

Firstly, counsellors can ensure that the environment is made as private and as relaxed as possible. I have already talked about checking the environment to make themselves as comfortable as possible. Now they need to consider it from the point of view of the person being counselled.

1 Will they be overheard?
2 Will they be seen by others?—Particularly important if they may show emotions.
3 Will anyone interrupt?
4 Can they get a drink to relieve tension easily?
5 Is there a phone that might ring?

The attitude of the counsellor

In my experience, this has more effect than anything else. If people are convinced that it is safe to talk with you, then they will even ignore environmental factors which might detract from that feeling of safety.

You create this 'safe environment' by being absolutely clear yourself that you are here to empower this person, that you will make no judgement, and will not use any information given to you in any other setting unless requested to by the individual. You also are calm and positive in your approach to the situation.

By using statements to themselves beforehand, and self-management techniques, counsellors can set themselves up to give the appropriate message of safety.

Explicit ground rules

The third way of making the person to be counselled feel safe is by making explicit some ground rules for the session. The counsellor may know these and take them for granted, but for the individual it is reassuring to have them stated aloud and guaranteed.

These ground rules may include:

- The right of the person being counselled to decide how far to take the topic and what action to take, if any.
- Confidentiality of anything discussed on both sides.
- No interruptions for a set time already arranged.
- No recriminations on other occasions for anything said during the session.

Feeling at ease Feeling that it is safe to talk openly will help the person being counselled to relax into the situation. It is also important to add in other small touches that will help to put the person at ease.

Environment Again, the environment can play a part in this. This can range from going to a quiet bar to talk, to making sure that the person being counselled has a reasonably comfortable seat, there is a drink available if it is wanted, an ash tray, a box of tissues, depending on the specific situation.

The attitude of the counsellor Again, this plays a major role in putting someone at ease. If you are relaxed and comfortable, it helps the person to be the same. You can also make sure that they are greeted and made welcome as a real individual, not as your next client on the list. Things like using the person's name, remarking on the weather, asking if he or she would like a drink, asking after the family, etc., are not just polite small talk. They are a way of acknowledging the individual, and also showing your own 'ordinariness'.

Allowing time to get ready Sometimes the individual will be in a state which will distract from the session in hand. They may have come to you straight from other pressing business and still have that in mind. They may have built up an aggressiveness as self-protection and may be very upset. The person may be flustered because someone stopped them on the way to you to make an urgent request. There are a wide variety of reasons for someone not being ready to use a counselling session well.

Just by suggesting that the individual takes five minutes to get ready, the counsellor is helping them to approach the session more constructively. It is the beginning of the message that they can make a difference for themselves and are not a victim of either circumstances or their own emotions.

This does not always work, of course, but it is surprising how often that five minutes can make the session more constructive and useful for both sides.

Peter came to me for a counselling session direct from a team briefing he had conducted. He arrived flustered, because he was a little late, and immediately started apologizing, saying this was typical of him. He then launched into some of the problems he had encountered in the team briefing.

I listened for a few minutes, then suggested that he went and got a cup of coffee, sat with a piece of paper, and noted down what he needed to remember from the team briefing. After that, I suggested that he took a deep breath and walked round the block.

> When he came back in, he was in a much better state, and ready to deal with his issues. The extra ten minutes had saved us both a lot of time, because he was now able to deal with what he wanted to discuss more constructively.

All these techniques for setting the right tone are simple and obvious. When we are feeling on form, they would be mostly automatic behaviour and common sense. But by spelling these out consciously we give workplace counsellors both confidence—they know they can already do these things and we are just endorsing—and a useful reminder. By making these important, we remind them not to skip them if they feel pressured, or forget them if something panics them. Common sense is least likely to be used when it is most needed—to offset a 'panic button'.

By giving these techniques some status, we are helping counsellors to use their common sense when they need it!

Being clear about the outcomes

I often think that the most useful piece of advice which I give to workplace counsellors is to stop trying to sort people out and solve their problems. Feeling that they have to take on this parental or expert role is a major source of doubt that they have the capability to be a good workplace counsellor.

Even if they *do* feel able to take on this role, I would strongly encourage them not to. A good workplace counsellor would not want to create the sort of dependency which this type of intervention brings about.

To increase confidence in those who have doubts, and to change the focus of those who feel they can sort everyone out, we need to spend a little time examining outcomes with them.

What are outcomes?

It is important to begin by explaining exactly what we mean by outcomes.

They are the immediate and ongoing results of the intervention.

I would stress this two-part perspective on outcomes.

Often we only think about the immediate result, and forget to take the longer-term view.

> An example of this would be the salesperson who manipulates the customer into a purchase that he or she is not really sure about. Immediately, the salesperson has improved sales figures. Longer term, return custom may have been lost, and even new custom through word-of-mouth.

This perspective helps to reinforce why 'quick-fix' solutions to problems are not a useful approach. The counsellor may have felt that the individual has been helped, and the individual may even agree. However, the longer-term perspective reminds us that the individual will not have learnt to solve their own problems in future, and instead will keep coming back to the counsellor for help. This puts an increasing burden on the counsellor to always have the right answer. If the solution does not work, the individual will not want to consult with the counsellor again, and the latter will have lost trust and respect.

Expressing outcomes

Most people think about the results of any interaction or situation to some extent. However, we are not usually well trained in how to express our outcomes in the most useful way.

Our unconscious is a powerful tool that we need to learn to use, and our formal education in Western culture does not usually teach us how to use it. Most people would recognize that we seem to be good at self-fulfilling prophecy. Yet we tend to use this ability to predict negative rather than positive results! For example, if we think a meeting is going to be difficult and inconclusive, it usually is.

It is therefore worth experimenting to see what happens if we change our prediction, and convince ourselves that a meeting is going to be useful and constructive! This is partly what we were working on in the section on beliefs in Chapter 7. We will add to it, when we come to setting outcomes.

Further to this, we often think about the results we do not want, and express a wish that we will not get them. For example, I may say to myself: 'I hope I do not end up annoying this person'. It is noticeable that we often seem to get the result we did not want, or, at best, we notice it starting to happen, and just manage to avert the disaster because we had thought about what we should do if it were to happen.

This is because we have focused our unconscious attention on the result we do not want, and so it automatically turns that result into another self-fulfilling prophecy.

We therefore need to express our outcomes in the positive: what we want, *not* what we do not want. We also need to express our desired outcomes, the results we would be pleased with, rather than the outcomes we fear we may get.

Types of outcomes

There are basically two types of outcomes:

- Product outcomes—things which are done as a result.
- Process outcomes—the way things are done and the way people relate.

Again, our normal practice tends to be to pay attention to the product outcomes and ignore the process outcomes. A typical product outcome for a counselling session may be: 'I want them to make a decision.' When we look at a longer-term perspective, and add in process outcomes we may find that we have a different outcome.

Process outcomes When we stop and consider how we want the session to go, we are likely to add in other outcomes, such as:

- We want them to feel good about making the decision.
- We want to enhance their personal empowerment.
- We want to feel that we have offered them a chance for some useful learning.

We all have our own versions of this list. What the process outcome gives us is a reminder that we need more than a practical result to feel that we have been successful. When we add to this the longer-term perspective, we may want to consider the ongoing work relationship with this individual, and their ability to use the approach in the future.

Prioritizing outcomes Having considered all the different angles of creating a description of the outcomes which will mean to them that they have been successful, counsellors can just check which are most important in this session.

When we have not considered the full range, we often assume that getting an immediate result matters most. However, when counsellors have considered short-term and long-term, product and process outcomes, they may find that they would give priority to the individual learning the process to solve his or her own issues, or to building the relationship.

Developing outcome-setting skills When we are helping counsellors to develop their skills in this area, it is useful to take them through these basic principles for setting outcomes, and then ask them to practise applying them to a specific likely session they will be having in the future, with a specific individual.

Ask counsellors to consider if the session is successful, how will they know? Give them the following categories:

1 The immediate action(s) they will take or result they will notice.
2 The immediate action(s) the person will take or difference they will make.
3 How they will feel at the end of the session.
4 How they will relate to the other person at the end of the session.
5 How the other person will feel at the end of the session.
6 What the effect longer term will be for them.
7 What the effect longer term will be for the other person.

The use of outcomes By going through this process with counsellors, we can help them to recognize the importance of the approach to counselling, and to appreciate that it calls upon their interpersonal skills and human qualities rather than their 'expert' or problem-solving skills.

Besides giving increased confidence to counsellors by clarifying for them their purpose in undertaking this session, their outcomes can also be used to start off the session. By saying what they believe will demonstrate that the session has been successful, counsellors can reassure the individual being counselled, by offering another form of parameter or guideline for the session.

The outcomes of the person being counselled
Importantly, the counsellor needs to check out if the individual's desired outcomes match with theirs. Often these have not been thought through beforehand, and the counsellor's outcomes will prompt the individual to consider their own more fully. They will also help to shift the individual from: 'I want you to solve my problem' into 'I want to feel that you have helped me to solve my problem'.

Dovetailing outcomes
If there is a mismatch in what the two parties want, then it is important to sort that out at the beginning of the session. The counsellor needs to make clear what is and what is not possible.

For example, the individual may insist that the counsellor should solve the problem. The counsellor may agree to offer a personal opinion as well as exploring the ideas the individual may have, while maintaining that the decision on the appropriate solution will be the individual's.

Where the expectation of the individual is beyond the willingness or capability of the counsellor, the latter needs to state this, and then offer how they can be useful. By clarifying outcomes in this way, the counsellor reduces the likelihood of difficulties in the session, and can therefore approach it with more confidence.

The previous section on clarifying outcomes leads neatly to consideration of the parameters of workplace counselling. In order to know what they can or cannot deal with within workplace counselling, counsellors have to stop and think beforehand about what is feasible.

Setting parameters
We have already examined some aspects of how to establish the parameters of the counselling session. To give counsellors confidence in their ability to handle the situation, it is worth taking a little time to gather the various threads together.

The principles of the session
I mentioned setting the ground rules in the section on setting the tone for the counselling session. There are certain principles which need to be explicit if both sides are to feel safe and comfortable.

Confidentiality
Both sides need to know that whatever is discussed is 'within these four walls'.

Intention to improve the situation
Both sides need to be clear that the purpose of the session is to help the person being counselled to reach their own conclusions.

Empowerment   Both sides need to recognize that the session is a part of the process of enabling the person to take responsibility for their own development.

The principles of   ● Confidentiality.
workplace   ● Intention to improve the situation.
counselling   ● Empowerment of the individual.

The principles are essential to excellent workplace counselling, and the counsellor needs to stop to consider whether he or she can fulfil these principles in the particular situation. If they feel that they cannot, then it is unfair on the person being counselled to continue.

Possible reasons may be:

● Pressure from the organization to produce a particular result.
● A personal dislike/distrust of the person being counselled.

In these instances, the counsellor should refer the person to someone else who would not experience the same problems.

The limitations of   Not feeling able to fulfil the principles may be one limitation on the
the session   session. If the counsellor is to effectively counsel the person then they must consider first whether there are other limitations which may require that they either acknowledge those limitations or refers the person to someone else from the start.

Limitations through   It is important to remember that we are all human, and have certain
personal values   core values that govern our thinking. It would be difficult for a priest to offer counsel without prejudice to someone who was considering leaving the Catholic Church. If you believe strongly that everyone needs a job to play their part in society, it would be difficult to offer counsel without prejudice to someone who was considering giving up their job and living off others or the state.

All those who engage in counselling need to stop and consider what their core values are, and if they may affect their willingness to work with the other person to find the conclusion that suits that person.

This can then be acknowledged and dealt with, either by referral to someone else, or just by making sure the individual knows your prejudice. The choice depends on the comfort on both sides with the situation. It is worth noting, by the way, that sometimes the person being counselled has chosen the particular counsellor because of the former's prejudice—the person wants to be influenced in a particular direction.

Limitations of context   The workplace counsellor is there to help others in the workplace to develop themselves so as to be more effective at work. If the person is having trouble deciding whether to move house or not, and wants some help, the issue needs to be checked against this basic criterion. Is their indecision affecting their performance? If so, what will make the most difference to improving that performance: making the decision or learning how to manage themselves more effectively at times of indecision?

It is up to the workplace counsellor to maintain the focus on work performance, and if he or she enjoys using their skills to help people on an individual basis, then that should take place in a different context. By making it clear that the overall concern is to enhance work performance, the workplace counsellor can feel that they have some control over the level to which the issues are taken, and avoids becoming the sympathetic person who is constantly being called to help others.

Limitations of time and place
There are also limitations of time and place available within the work context. The workplace counsellor is also fulfilling other roles and responsibilities and needs to feel that they can control the time spent on counselling. Professional counsellors will allow a limited time per person, and keep strictly to that time. Workplace counsellors can certainly do the same. They may also need to point out that the environment is not ideal, but it is all that is available.

By establishing time parameters, counsellors can keep this aspect of their work in perspective, rather than feeling obliged to respond to requests for help immediately and for as long as is demanded, to prove they care.

Limitations of personal comfort
The last area where counsellors need to consider their parameters is the area of their personal comfort. They will not function effectively as counsellors if they feel uncomfortable or stressed because of the issue under consideration, or the reaction of the person being counselled.

Their discomfort may be caused by the subject—for example, someone who has just been appointed may feel uncomfortable dealing with someone who is being made redundant—or by the emotional reactions, such as those of someone who has been bereaved.

By acknowledging this discomfort and proposing that someone else would be more useful, the workplace counsellors are showing respect for the individual, by not pretending that they can be effective, while trying to manage the adverse effect on themselves. Most people will appreciate the honesty of this admission.

Moreover, the workplace counsellors who know that they can express a limitation on this basis, and refer the person, as part of good practice, will often be capable of handling more than they thought possible!

Using the parameters

Once the workplace counsellors have considered their own parameters for counselling, they can use them to clarify ground rules for the individual being counselled.

They can also use them as a yardstick within the session, to help them to decide sensibly if they need to stop the session and propose referral to someone else. This will protect them from getting caught up in something that they feel they cannot handle, and help them to recognize that to continue when feeling like that is not useful to them or the other person.

Referral

I have suggested several times that workplace counsellors may need to refer someone on. It is important for them to know that they have specific possibilities available, so that they are not deserting the person they want to help. Instead they are actually offering that help by referring the person to a more appropriate or useful source of help.

Referral within the organization

The first source of referral may be within the organization. There are two types of source here. The first is to people with a specialist knowledge or experience. This may be the doctor responsible for occupational health, the person who specializes in career development opportunities within personnel, or even the senior manager who has the authority to instigate a structural change which that person needs.

The other source of referral is to other workplace counsellors who may be more appropriate, either because they are more experienced or because they will not experience the same limitations, for example in the area of personal values.

If workplace counsellors have the opportunity to think through their own possible sources of referral within the organization, then they will be better prepared should the need arise.

Referral to outside agencies

The other source of referral is to specialist agencies outside the organization who deal with specific issues. These may include such people as professional counsellors, or agencies who deal with bereavement, gender issues, careers advice, health issues, personal development opportunities and so on.

When training workplace counsellors I would usually give them the opportunity to identify for themselves the issues where outside referral sources would be useful, and then to collect between them the relevant information and contacts. They then have most of the information at their fingertips if they need it, and also know how to go about finding out who could help if a need for referral they have not previously encountered occurs.

In this chapter I have concentrated on ways of building confidence in workplace counsellors which can be broadly described as preparatory work. These steps will give them the feeling of being in control of the situation and allow them to be at their best as they enter the counselling session. We now need to consider how we can enable them to handle the session itself effectively.

Key points

- Confidence in the ability to be a workplace counsellor is increased by identifying the requisite skills and qualities and practising their application.
- By devising a checklist of skills and qualities of an excellent workplace counsellor, people have the chance to recognize that there are some that they already have.
- Knowing how to set the right tone for the counselling session gives counsellors more chance of performing well. This is achieved by:
  — making the person being counselled feel safe through ensuring the environment is conducive, giving the appropriate message about your intentions as counsellor, and having explicit ground rules;
  — making the person being counselled feel at ease, through the comfort of the environment, and allowing them to make themselves comfortable and ready.
- Clarifying the outcomes of counselling is crucial to the confidence of counsellors. By learning to consider both product and process outcomes, they become more confident in their ability to succeed. They can also clear up misunderstandings about outcomes with the individual before they start.
- The counsellor needs to clarify the parameters of the session, for themselves and the other person, concerning confidentiality, intention of counsellor, and the overall aim of empowerment.
- Limitations also need to be clarified, in terms of personal values, the context, time and place available, and personal comfort of the counsellor.
- Counsellors are more comfortable with recognizing limiting parameters if they have sources of referral.

These steps are all essential preparation to enable workplace counsellors to feel more confident that they can fulfil the role.

9 Structuring a counselling session

In this chapter, we will look at the key skills involved in giving workplace counselling. These are all skills which most people have already to some degree. Our task as trainers is to increase people's conscious awareness of applying the skill and of its usefulness in being an effective counsellor.

How do counsellors help?

The guidance which the workplace counsellor gives is guidance on how to structure and organize thoughts and feelings in order to come to a useful and feasible conclusion which the person can act on.

It is literally acting as a guide to help the person to make their own journey successfully. This may involve pointing out that there are alternative routes, giving relevant information, or just helping the person to notice when they are in unsafe territory or when an attractive alternative has been spotted but dismissed because the person thinks it cannot be used.

The process of counselling

In order to do this form of guidance well, we first need to find out all we can about the perspective, needs, and preferences of the person being counselled. This means that any counselling session will start by finding out as much information as possible about their present situation and how they would like to change it.

Finding out information

The counsellor needs to gather information on two levels:

1 Factual information.
2 Affective or 'soft' information.

Finding out the facts about the particular issue is obviously important, but it is vital in offering guidance to be able to find out the feelings, values and beliefs which the person brings to the issue and its resolution.

Without awareness of these, the counsellor will not be able to help the person through to a useful conclusion, since it is these, rather than the facts that are likely to have most effect in determining our actions. Rational conclusions can be worked out without much help—it is where feelings are involved that our rationality is not enough.

It is also important to remember that the most useful conclusions may not be the most obvious rational ones. The counsellor therefore needs to find out how the person reacts to possible solutions, rather than assume that if the solution 'makes sense' to him or her, it is bound to be useful.

How to find out

There are obvious ways to find out: we need to ask questions and listen carefully. For most people, however, the way in which questions are asked, and the levels of listening they do are not enough to elicit the degree of information required to usefully counsel.

Questioning techniques

Most managers and personnel officers will already have come across information on questioning techniques through development in other areas of their job, such as interviewing skills, and will know that open questions are more useful than closed questions.

Yet when people actually start to question other people, they usually fall into the common traps of making assumptions, and implying judgements. People make statements like: 'Yes, I find I'm not as settled as I used to be as well. I suppose that you are worried about the short-term contracts we now have, too?' The person may just have stated that they are feeling less secure in the job, but the questioner has immediately assumed that he or she knows why rather than finding out that person's perspective. If the person then agrees with the questioner, the latter will believe that the issue has actually been identified because it makes sense to them in their own experience. Yet this may only be a small part of the cause of insecurity, and they may end up by pursuing solutions to only a small part of the problem.

Being judgemental

There is also the common use of the question 'why' to elicit information. It is unfortunate that this question is not as useful as it may seem, since it is the most commonly used question in the English language.

When someone asks you 'why' you unconsciously tend to become slightly defensive. After all, its most frequent use is because someone thinks you have not made sense, or even that you are wrong. It therefore tends to elicit justifications, explanations or defences of your position. By reacting like this, you are building your case for the position you are taking rather than giving the other person more information. Even if the questioner's intention is just to find out more, you will tend unconsciously to assume that the other person is being judgemental, and give a somewhat defensive answer.

Useful questions   If we are going to offer guidance, we need to find out about the person's perspective, and the different aspects of the issue from their point of view. We cannot afford to make any assumptions, or to create some form of defensiveness.

It is therefore sensible to ask questions which are likely to effectively elicit the information we need. Rather than 'Why did that happen?', we can ask 'What exactly happened?' or 'How exactly did that happen?' The first question will check if what we assume they mean is accurate. The second question will find out what they see as leading up to the issue and causing it.

> Just notice the difference in the information if the person is stating that he gave up a college course. 'Why did that happen?' produces: 'Well it wasn't because I wasn't able to do the studies, I just didn't have time, what with a young family and work.' 'What exactly happened?' produces: 'I found it hard to balance the different demands of college, work, and family, and the college didn't take any account of your personal circumstances. When I asked for an extension for a piece of work, they told me I had had enough leeway, and should consider deferring until I could do the course properly.'

Two other useful questions for eliciting more information on their perspectives are:

- 'What does *x* mean to you?'
- 'What would be a specific example of *x*?'

These questions make sure that we do not assume that we understand. In my experience, the answers to these useful questions are so often different to what I would have expected, that they have become vital tools to ensure that I accurately identify what needs to be considered before we leap into conclusions.

What do you want?   The other side of finding out is to make sure that as counsellor you are really clear about the results and effects that the person wants. I have already considered the subject of outcomes in detail in Chapter 8, in relation to the counselling session itself.

The same principle can be applied to helping people to find the outcome they want in relation to their particular issue.

Often people are clear about their issue, yet unclear about how it can be resolved, and that is what has brought them into the counselling situation. What the counsellor is there to offer is help in resolving the issue, and it is therefore vital to find out what they would see as resolution.

Again, we cannot afford to make assumptions. What people usually offer in response to the question 'What do you see as the resolution?' is the unsatisfactory answer they have come up with so far, or 'I don't know'.

The counsellor can help them to become clearer about exactly what they do want as outcomes by finding out more.

Useful questions   When counselling, we can begin by asking people to consider the three parts of an outcome: What result do you want? What short-term effect do you want? What long-term effect do you want?

This will immediately help them to identify the consequences of their desired results, and often help them to recognize what made their resolution seem unsatisfactory. It is important to encourage people to express their ideal outcomes, rather than the limited version that they think is possible. The dissatisfaction they feel with their own answer is usually because it would not really work for them.

> The person referred to earlier who had given up a college course several years before, wanted to try to get a qualification. The conclusion he had come to was that he would have to get a less demanding job if he were to be able to do this, based on his previous experiences of the strains of trying to fit everything in.
>
> When asked what results he wanted, ideally, he said he wanted to gain a qualification and keep his family life and his job, which he enjoyed. When asked what effect he wanted, he said he wanted to be able to manage it all better than last time, and have support from home and the workplace. When asked about long-term effects, he said that he wanted to prove to himself his capability, be recognized for his ability at work, and have improved relationships at home through his experience.
>
> As he went through this, as counsellor I needed to prompt him to leave the 'but I can't' statements for later in the session. I also prompted him to acknowledge the effects he wanted at work and at home, so he had considered the full outcomes. My questions included: 'How do you want to feel as you get this result?' 'How do you want others to react?' 'How do you want this to pay off for you in the future?' What we had by the end of this was a very different resolution from the one he had initially presented: 'I need help in finding a less demanding job, so I can go and get a qualification.'

Beyond limitations Sometimes we need to prompt people beyond their limited view of what is possible by checking out their underlying desire. In this instance I could have begun with questions like: 'What makes you feel you need a less demanding job?' or 'What do you think a qualification will give you?' Either of these would provoke answers which would help me to understand what the person really wanted as outcomes.

Priorities Finally, we may need to check what matters most to the people concerned. When we have encouraged them to define their ideal outcomes, they may realize that the most important thing to them is not the result itself, but some of the effects.

In order to check out priorities we need to ask: 'What matters most to you about this?' or 'What is important to you about this?' In the example I have cited, the man wanted recognition of his ability and ambition, and to become better at managing the various demands on him so he felt less stressed.

Is this counselling?

So far in the process, all we have considered is ways of finding out more information about both the issue and the person's perspective on the ideal resolution. It may seem that we have not even begun offering guidance.

Yet by asking useful questions, and finding out more information, the counsellor is guiding the thought processes of the person being counselled, and helping to clarify what the issue is really about for them.

I have had many people at this stage in the process turn round and say: 'Oh, so that's what it's about! What I really need to do then is …' In other words, this finding out process has been enough for them to finish off the process themselves. Since my intention is to empower the person to resolve their own issues, I am delighted if this happens! They also now have a way of clarifying the issue for themselves by asking themselves the sorts of questions which I have used.

Summary of useful questions for finding out

- What exactly happened?
- How did that happen?
- What exactly does … mean to you?
- What would be an example of …?
- How exactly did you …?
- What result do you want ideally?
- What short-term effects do you want ideally?
- What long-term effects do you want ideally?
- How do you want to feel as you get this result?
- How do you want others to react?

- What makes you feel that . . .?
- What do you think would give you . . .?
- What matters most to you about this?
- What is important to you about this?

Practising the questions   I usually ask participants to practise using these questions with each other, so they have an opportunity to experience the different effect that they have, as well as how tempting it is to make assumptions and lead people to your own right answer!

Using the questions effectively   These questions are only effective if they are used well. This means that the counsellor has the intention of enabling the person to explore their own issue. If you want to use these questions to be judgemental or to make assumptions or to lead someone to your answer, you can—it comes across through the tone of voice, the way of asking the questions, and through what you choose to question about.

The questions alone are not enough to guarantee a useful process. We therefore need to base them in the context of the overall approach to counselling, and the skills which provide that approach. We have considered the preparatory stages of this in Chapter 8. Now we will examine the approach needed within the counselling situation itself.

Giving attention

It seems obvious to state that we need to give attention to the person being counselled, if we are to offer useful counselling. This skill is fundamental to effectively relating with others, and if we want to know what is going on with the other person, we need to give full attention.

Yet most of us do not use full attention with others—we filter the information they are giving through our own perceptions, and take from it only what we expect.

What is full attention?   When parents have a baby, they are likely to adopt full attention. There are no words to tell them what the baby wants or needs, so they have to rely on their ability to give full attention.

They pay attention to how the baby sounds, what its body language suggests, and they also use their intuition and their hearts to bring richness to the attention. And parents can be remarkably good at 'second-guessing' what the baby wants!

The distraction of content   Once there is language, we become distracted from this multi-level attention, and tend to get caught up in what the person is saying, rather than the sound of it, the look of the person, and what our hearts and intuition are telling us.

We pay attention to the words, and can often repeat them verbatim to prove that we have paid attention—but we have missed the full meaning by ignoring the other levels of attention.

We also get distracted into our own interpretations of the words: whether we agree or not; if we have had similar experiences or feelings; what the words mean to us. This can stop us from noticing how the other person's perspective is different, so we make assumptions. It can also lead us to make judgements rather than appreciate their perspective.

Practising full attention

By using full attention, the counsellor will find out a different and vital quality of information—the feelings and values which are underlying what the person is saying. It is this information which will enable the counsellor to offer useful guidance to the person, in the majority of cases.

Furthermore, full attention is respectful of the individual and his or her world. It does not lead to assumptions or judgements, but rather explores the person's perspective. When receiving full attention, people unconsciously feel safe and respected, and will tend to react by being more open and honest because they lose the fear of being judged.

Finally, full attention will give the counsellor an informed basis from which to choose what to elicit more information about, which angles to pursue. He or she will follow up the feelings about what is being said rather than the content.

> An example of the difference it makes is the scenario where you have asked someone to do something, and she has said 'all right' in that tone of voice, with that manner which tells you she is reluctant, and even unlikely to follow it through. Yet you take the words as the message, and act as if she has genuinely agreed. When she does not do it, or does it badly, you say that you 'knew' this would happen, and are angry with her. I believe that it is ourselves we should be angry with! If giving full attention in this scenario, the behaviour would immediately prompt you to check out the cause of the reluctance, and possible ways of getting past that obstacle. You would respond to the real message, and avoid unnecessary resentment on both sides.

Non-judgemental attitude

By giving full attention, the counsellor increases the likelihood of being able to be non-judgemental. Because he or she is fully engaged in the other person's perspective and reactions, the counsellor reduces the tendency to interpret and judge that person from his or her own perspective and values.

It is important to be aware that we do have this tendency and to consciously keep it in check. When someone says something, our first thoughts tend to be: 'I agree' or 'that's wrong' or 'I don't see it that way' or 'that won't work.' These are all judgements, and even if we do not voice them out loud, they 'show' in our unconscious reactions, and the other person picks up the message.

How to be non-judgemental

The easiest way to achieve this is not to try to stop yourself making judgements. This just means that you try to suppress the thoughts as they arise, and they will still tend to affect your reactions unconsciously.

It is more effective if you give your mind something else to do. For example, you can decide to be curious about how this person 'ticks' or choose to notice how differently they approach things—both these will automatically switch off the judgement.

Noticing cues

When giving attention, we automatically become more aware of cues that people give us. It is worth noticing what type of cues we need to follow up if we are going to really help them to structure their thought process.

Above all we need to look for the mismatch—where words say one thing and the body says something different. This is often where the crux of the problem and the resolution lies. By simply remarking that they do not seem to be fully committed to their statement, and asking what would make a difference, we can often help them to shift considerable ground.

Also we can notice when there is a significant change in people—their voice tone changes, they shift physically, their colour changes, their gestures change. These usually indicate that something important is going on, and are worth checking out, again just by asking them such questions as: 'How is this important to you?' or even 'What's going through your mind at the moment?'

> Stephanie had stated clearly that she wanted to improve her relationship with her colleagues. When she gave examples of the situations she wanted to change, there was a distinct difference between her unconscious reactions to ones which involved a particular colleague, and the rest. Her facial expression and her voice tone changed, and she became quite fidgety. When I remarked on this, she blushed, and then said, 'Well, I do worry more about what she thinks of me, because I really admire her, and I think that she thinks I am stupid.'

This type of noticing is often invaluable to people being counselled because they are quite unaware of these unconscious reactions, and so do not realize that they have 'found' something useful until you draw their attention to it.

Respect and sympathy

In many ways, I have already covered the ways in which we elicit these qualities in ourselves towards others. By setting up our intentions and outcomes for the session, we are setting the frame for the qualities of respect and sympathy to show. By giving full attention and being non-judgemental we enhance these qualities in ourselves.

They still deserve to be explicitly considered, because they are two qualities which affect significantly the response we get from the other person.

Sympathy

I remember a physically handicapped person I encountered saying to me: 'We want sympathy, not pity.' Sympathy means 'feeling with' someone, caring about how it is for them, without feeling sorry from them. It comes from our hearts, and is very quickly transmitted to the other person. My caring is about fellow-feeling; this is another human being doing their best to make it through this somewhat confusing thing called life.

It makes people feel you appreciate them and their predicament and would be glad to help them find a way through, rather than that you are just 'doing your job'.

Sympathy finds its natural and general expression if you simply allow yourself to appreciate the other person's viewpoint. It is not necessarily about saying 'Oh what a shame' or 'You poor thing'. I have a teacher who has said things to me like, 'Come on, don't be pathetic. You can do something about this.' Yet I have sensed his sympathy as he said it, and found it somehow comforting.

Respect

Showing respect for others is another quality which cannot be taught, because there is no one way of showing respect. Reminding yourself that if we treat others as we would wish to be treated, we are likely to be respectful is a useful technique.

Respecting others means respecting what matters to them and allowing their viewpoints as having validity, whether we agree or not. The techniques we have considered so far all contribute to helping us to have that mind-set.

When the approach I have just outlined is used in applying the questions for finding out information, then the counsellor has established clearly the tone of the counselling session. What I have said so far may already have helped people to be able to solve issues by themselves. If they are still struggling with how to achieve the outcome they want, then the counsellor can help them to think through and find various strategies which would move them in the direction they want to go.

Helping someone to find ways of achieving their outcome

Once we have clarified exactly what the issue is, and also what the person would like as the outcome, we tend immediately to work out how to resolve the problem. We know what 'the answer' is, and now we have to try to get the person to recognize it. Alternatively, we may be convinced that the person's ideal outcome is not feasible, and that he or she will have to put up with a different resolution.

But this is *our* perspective, and is based on *our* beliefs and experience. The task as counsellor is *not* to give our conclusion, but to help people to think through possibilities for themselves.

Putting on one side your own answer

So the first thing the counsellor has to do is to put aside their own conclusion, so that it does not affect the way they guide the person to a resolution.

You can do this by reminding yourself that this person has a different perspective on things from you, and may well come to a different conclusion. It is helpful to think of a time when someone 'solved' a problem for you but the solution was not useful for you. This will help you to recognize how that type of 'guidance' can have the opposite effect to the one you want to achieve.

You have the opportunity to learn here. You can enjoy discovering how different or how similar a person's conclusion is to yours.

Where are they up to?

Once the counsellor's conclusion has been put on one side, a start can be made on the process of helping the person to structure their own thinking. First of all the counsellor will need to find out what this person has already considered.

A simple question, like: 'What options have you already considered?' will elicit this information. These are ideas which may have been dismissed as not being feasible or not being enough to make the difference the person wanted. As they are expressed, the person will tend to say, 'I thought of x, but . . .,' and give a reason for dismissing it.

If the counsellor is paying full attention, he or she will notice that these reasons for dismissal will fall into different categories:

1 'I know that's sensible, but it doesn't appeal to me.'
2 'I'd like to be able to do this, but I don't think it's possible.'
3 'I'd like this alternative, but I see obstacles.'

Is it possible?

If the reasons for dismissal of the idea fall into the second category, the counsellor can follow up, by asking, 'What would make it possible for you to ...?' or 'What would make you feel able to ...?' These questions are designed to encourage people to reconsider those alternatives and use their creativity to come up with ways of making them work. The questions assume that it *is* possible to do it, but that the person has not yet identified how.

Overcoming obstacles   If the reasons for dismissal of the idea fall into the third category, then the counsellor can help someone to consider how to overcome the obstacles. Questions like, 'So how could you deal with this obstacle?' or 'How could you change this?' will encourage the person to consider possible strategies.

As the counsellor gets responses to these questions, he or she may be tempted to stop if the person has identified a possible strategy. I would encourage them to ask 'And what else would work?' or 'How else might you do this?', so that the person has a fall-back strategy if the first one does not work.

What can I do?   This is also a useful technique for dealing with answers which are based on something changing beyond the person's control, such as: 'if I won the lottery ...'. It means that we do not dismiss that idea, while continuing to explore more controllable possibilities. If the answer refers to a significant change in themselves or in someone else involved, then the counsellor needs to ask: 'So how can you begin to effect this change?' This is obvious when the subject is themselves, but more of a challenge when the subject is someone else. It puts the responsibility for evoking a different behaviour back on the person who wants the change, and empowers that person to consider ways of eliciting a different reaction.

That's sensible   You may have noticed that I have not picked up on responses from the first category. They are usually the answers which someone thinks should be given, rather than ones which will work for them. Unless the answer 'sparks' something in the person, it will be unlikely to work well for them as a resolution.

I don't know   Sometimes the person has not considered any options, or has dismissed them all under the first category. The counsellor can begin to help the person to think of some options by asking one of the following questions:

● 'So what might help you to achieve the outcome you want?'
● 'How do you think you could resolve this?'
● 'How could you change this to what you want?'

Use 'what else' or 'how else' if the person has already considered some options.

Again, notice how these questions prompt the person to 'search' their creativity for more possibilities rather than accepting that there are no more answers.

When they are stuck If someone cannot come up with any other options, and has reached an impasse, then the counsellor can help them to tap into their intuition by asking: 'If you were someone who could resolve this, how would you go about it?' By using this question, the counsellor shifts them from their own limitations to considering how other people resolve similar issues, which will extend their ideas.

Sometimes they are stuck because they are not sure if they really want to make the effort. In this case, it is worth asking, 'What would make it worth while for you to . . .?', so that they uncover their own motivators. The counsellor can then revert to some of the other questions to guide their thinking.

It's not possible Of course, there are occasions when the person's ideal outcome does genuinely seem to be beyond reach. When this occurs, then the counsellor can still help to find ways of dealing with it.

There are two routes to explore:

● How to react differently.
● How to start moving towards the ideal.

Reacting differently When something is not how we want it to be, we have an adverse reaction to it. Even if we cannot change it, we can always change our reaction to it.

By asking the person, 'How can you change its effect on you?', the counsellor can prompt them into considering taking control of themselves in the situation, so that they no longer feel the 'victim of circumstance'.

Moving towards the ideal When the person cannot find a way to achieve an ideal, they are often inclined to give up altogether.

The counsellor can help the person to find ways of at least moving closer to the ideal than at present. This will help them to get some momentum and may well be enough to help them to then go on to achieve the ideal after all.

'What would make a positive difference to the present state of things?' 'How could you make some difference which moved you closer to what you want?' These are the types of question which will prompt the person to find ways of at least beginning to move in the right direction. Again, the counsellor can ask, 'And what else would make a difference?', so that the person has several strategies to help themselves to move.

Summary of questions to help someone find useful strategies

- What options have you already considered?
- What would make it possible for you to ...?
- What would make you feel able to ...?
- How could you deal with this obstacle?
- How could you change this?
- And what else would work?
- And how else could you do this?
- How can you begin to effect this change in *x*?
- What might help you achieve the outcome you want?
- How do you think you could resolve this?
- How could you change this to what you want?
- If you were someone who could resolve this, how would you go about it?
- What would make it worth while for you to ...?
- How can you change its effect on you?
- What would make a positive difference to the current state of things?
- How could you make some difference which would bring you closer to what you want?

Turning thought into action

The final stage of the counselling session is when the counsellor ensures that the person will take some action on their resolution. All that the person has come up with so far will be ideas and possibilities, and it is much more likely that they will act on these if prompted to consider the specific actions to be taken *before* the person gets distracted by the return to the working environment.

Here the counsellor can ask, 'What will be your first step?' or 'What are you going to do now?' and confirm with the individual how they will begin to make a difference.

Counselling for empowerment

You may have noticed that the approach throughout this framework puts responsibility for making the required difference firmly in the court of the individual who has the issue. All the questions are designed to help the individual identify how they can change their own story.

Workplace counsellors are thereby using the opportunity of a counselling session to enhance the individual's ability to take control of and responsibility for their own destiny. By structuring the session with the different stages of finding out, exploring, and pinning down to action, the person is offered a model of how to follow those stages through.

This can be made explicit, by offering people copies of questions they can use for themselves on other issues. These questions also encourage people to use their intuition and ability to create new alternatives, and so have a further pay-off, developing those abilities which are crucial to both individuals and organizations in a changing world.

Finishing a counselling session

When the counsellor has worked through the issue with the person, he or she may consider the work finished. The excellent workplace counsellor will be aware that the final stage of the session is not identifying the action the person is going to take, but reviewing the process with the person.

Reviewing the process

By just briefly running through the stages again, reminding the person of how they have dealt with their own issue, the counsellor adds value to what has happened:

1 By affirming and reminding the person of their own answers.
2 By giving recognition to the person's ability to sort themselves out.
3 By bringing the person's attention to the process as well as the content, so that they can apply the process to a different context.

Completion

Finally the counsellor can conclude the session in a supportive and empowering way. This will enable the person to leave feeling that he or she has grown through the experience, and that the counsellor is not 'just doing a job'.

Offering support

At this stage, the counsellor may offer support. This can be through a statement, such as: 'I wish you well in achieving this, and I'd like to hear about your progress.'

The counsellor may also feel it is appropriate to ask if there is any way they can help or support the person, or to offer specific help which is within the counsellor's remit, such as endorsing an application for a course to the training department.

Remembering the whole person

At the very end of the session, both counsellor and person being counselled will benefit from reminders that they are both rounded individuals who have been fulfilling particular roles for a short period of time. Regaining perspective of the session as a very small part of what is going on is useful, and the counsellor can prompt this by referring to normal things as they part.

By knowing how to structure the session usefully, and how to ask effective questions, the workplace counsellor will feel more confident of their ability to handle the situation. When it is also realized that the approach required to make the session successful is not something alien, but rather the natural reaction of one sympathetic and interested human being to another, then the counsellor is more likely to feel that it is something they can do.

Key points
- Counsellors help by guiding people in structuring and organizing their thoughts and feelings in order to come to a useful conclusion.
- The process of counselling begins with finding out information.
- It is vital to avoid making assumptions about the issue or jumping to judgements about the person.
- There are specific questions which are useful in helping the counsellor to find out accurately what the issue is, and how the person would want it to be resolved.
- The process of finding out is a crucial part of helping the person to organize their thoughts and feelings.
- Questioning only works well when the counsellor uses the right approach. This involves giving full attention, being non-judgemental, and noticing cues—all skills which can be developed.
- This personal attitude of respect for the individual and sympathy for their predicament is vital and can be consciously chosen.
- Having clarified the issue and the desired result, the counsellor can then help the person to work out how to achieve the result.
- Use of questions to help people find ways of moving towards their outcome is more useful and empowering than solving their problem for them. Questions can be used to:
  - check what they have already considered;
  - help them to reconsider possibilities;
  - help them to identify ways of overcoming obstacles;
  - guide them to take responsibility rather than be victims of circumstance;
  - recognize the difference between what they want and what they think they should want;
  - help them to find new ideas when they are stuck;
  - guide them towards changing their reaction;
  - help them find first steps towards change.
- Finally the counsellor can use questions to help them to turn good ideas into specific actions they can commit to and take. The counsellor may at this stage offer support.
- The process of a counselling session is completed when the counsellor has prompted a review of the session, and also helped them both put the session into perspective. Using this process, the counsellor is empowering the individual to take personal responsibility, and helping them to learn how to do so.

10 Giving direction in counselling

In Chapter 9, the 'script' for the counsellor was kept to a minimum. Most of the time, the counsellor was merely a sympathetic listener and questioner. In this chapter we will consider the occasions when it is appropriate for the counsellor to give direction to the person being counselled.

The dangers of direction

When I am training workplace counsellors, I put the emphasis on the skills of paying attention and asking useful questions for several reasons:

- *These are the primary skills of counselling for empowerment* It is through development of this approach that the workplace counsellor will become most effective in enabling others to develop themselves.
- *These skills are within the reach of most people* They recognize them, and know that they can use them in other situations, so feel more confident about developing them for this context.
- *We all have a tendency to think giving advice equates with being helpful* The would-be workplace counsellor believes that he or she needs to know the answers, rather than the process and sees counselling as the same as solving problems.
- *Giving advice requires higher level skills than most workplace counsellors will have, if it is to be effective and useful to the other person* Human problems, as opposed to practical problems, are so individual, and also usually non-rational, that the adviser needs significant experience and development to be able to help.

Being helpful

Most people like the idea of helping other people. It gives them a sense of satisfaction and of being needed. The implication of being a counsellor is that you are there to help people and so the temptation to give advice or tell them your answer is increased.

When I introduce the idea of useful questions to a group, I usually offer an example of the sort of issue I want them to use to practise the questions. Without fail, people begin to offer solutions to my issue, almost as soon as I have finished saying it. Despite the fact that I have introduced it as a subject for them to practise asking questions with, they cannot resist 'being helpful'. It is a very powerful illustration of how strong the tendency is in us, and why it is so important to train workplace counsellors in helping others in a different way by structuring the process.

Giving advice

When we believe that we are more experienced or know more in some way, most of us will be glad to advise others. This is not only a way of being helpful, it is also a demonstration of our experience or knowledge. Within Western culture, being an 'expert' has been highly valued, so we enjoy the feeling of knowing better than someone else.

In the context of counselling for empowerment, this 'knowing better' is often disempowering rather than empowering.

Firstly, there is the danger of giving advice which may be useful from your perspective, but which is less useful from the other person's perspective, or even limiting their options. The counsellor needs to have highly developed awareness of the other person's perspective in order to be able to gauge the usefulness of their advice to that person.

Secondly, even if the advice would be useful, it may still be disempowering. If the counsellor does give advice and it is useful, this stops the person working out solutions for themselves—they do not need to, because the counsellor has already done it. They then become dependent on the counsellor to be wise for them, rather than learning how to uncover their own wisdom. The counsellor, then, needs to be able to assess whether their advice would help the person to continue to develop their self-awareness, or if it would create dependency. He or she also needs to be self-resourceful enough not to want to create such dependency.

However, there are ways in which workplace counsellors can usefully give direction, and once they have developed the basic skills, they will be able to recognize when it would be appropriate.

Giving factual information

The workplace counsellor is in a different position to the professional counsellor. He or she is also someone who fulfils other functions in the organization, and has knowledge and experience of the context in which the individual is operating.

Sometimes individuals would be able to progress towards their desired outcome much more quickly if they were to be given information which the counsellor has, and they have not.

If the counsellor holds back this information, and continues to ask the individual how they could deal with the situation, the session loses credibility on both sides. Someone once said to me: 'He asked me how I could find out who controls the budget relating to this issue, and I told him that I would ask my manager, if he weren't so busy counselling me!' The essential check that the counsellor needs to make is: 'Would this information help this person to progress, or would it limit their learning and empowerment?'

Information can be very empowering. Telling someone how a system or process works can be the information needed so that they can concentrate on developing the skills to use that system well. The counsellor can also give added value by pointing out how the person could find out the factual information without talking to the fact-holder.

Taking action

In a similar vein, there are circumstances where the workplace counsellor is also the person who can usefully take action to help the individual. To continue to ask the individual to find ways of achieving their outcome without acknowledging this, is having the opposite effect to that intended.

Taking action through responsibility

Where someone's progress will be achieved much more easily by having the manager's or personnel officer's active support and sometimes even intervention, then it is appropriate to offer that support.

Examples would include:

- Endorsement of an application for a training programme.
- Managerial support for bringing up the proposal for a rearrangement of the office environment in a team meeting.
- Helping to convince a busy head of department that this person should have the opportunity to meet with him or her.

This active support is what a manager or personnel officer could offer automatically if the person came to request it and could demonstrate how it would help the latter to achieve a developmental outcome. The fact that the counsellor has helped the person to work through to this conclusion does not mean that he or she cannot then help in this way.

Taking action as development

Where someone is tackling what for them is a big issue, which requires development on several levels, the counsellor may give active help to make it easier for them to achieve some of their development, rather than give up on all of it. This is an interim step, to help a person to continue to develop and become empowered. We do not expect a child to go directly from riding a tricycle to riding a bicycle. We usually give them stabilizers at first, to help them in the transition of learning to balance for themselves. Similarly the counsellor may act as advocate to help towards learning to take full responsibility for themselves.

> I was working with someone on overcoming his fear of interviews. He had found for himself strategies which would, he felt, make it much easier to be interviewed. He was still worried that he would sabotage himself by raising the fears again before he actually went in to be interviewed. I volunteered to accompany him to the interview to help him keep in a good state beforehand, so that he could perform well in the actual interview. This allowed him to concentrate on doing well in the interview, and once he had evidence that he could perform well, we could consider how he could maintain his confidence beforehand without the 'stabilizer' of me with him.

Taking action to benefit the individual

In both these types of taking action, the decision to do so comes from awareness on the part of the counsellor that it will contribute to the person's development, rather than disempower them and lead to dependency and a lessening of self-worth.

It is vital that the counsellor can make this distinction, to avoid the danger of taking action to make themselves feel useful, rather than for the benefit of the person's development.

Useful interventions

Within the counselling process, there are occasions where the counsellor can help the person to continue in working out a resolution by offering an intervention. This may be a comment, an example or a reminder and will usually apply when the individual has reached a sticking point in the process.

All of us have points at which we cannot go beyond the tramline we are presently on. It is like the person who cannot find where he put his car keys—someone else may spot them immediately, or help him to remember, by making a few suggestions. There are times when the counsellor's intervention can help the person to regain a useful perspective.

When someone is 'stuck'

When the person cannot find a way through a particular obstacle, then the counsellor may help them to start thinking creatively again, by offering some examples of others who have gone past similar obstacles, or of other times when this person might have overcome an obstacle which may have similar features.

Counter-examples

> When someone told me that she could not even consider how she could get the promotion she wanted because the post required that the applicant had a degree, I reminded her that the new sales director did not have a degree, and also talked about a colleague who was pursuing a part-time degree course. I then pointed out that this requirement was not true of all companies.

These examples are enough to start them off again on considering how they might achieve the outcome they want. By offering a range of counter-examples, some of which are within their own experience, you can help them recognize that the obstacle is not an absolute fact.

Reference experiences

When people are struggling with how to cope with a dramatic change in their life, either professionally or personally, I will often talk about other times when most of us experience change, and do manage to cope with it, such as leaving home, setting up home with someone, having a child, moving house. They can then refer back to a personal example where they did manage change quite well, and identify how they made it easier for themselves to cope. This learning can then be applied to the present situation.

Use of stories

Sometimes it is useful if the counsellor can use a personal story to help the person get past the feeling of being 'stuck'. It is important to be clear about the type of personal story required if it is to be a useful intervention. When someone is describing something we relate to, we are tempted to tell our story about it, particularly if we solved it. The story is only useful if:

- It demonstrates recognition of what it feels like to be 'stuck'. We want the person to feel valued as they are, not stupid because they cannot solve it.
- It illustrates the *process* of resolution, rather than just the answer. By being able to show how we resolved it, what helped, our thinking processes, etc., we give the person some ideas of how to get moving again.

People often tell me that they just have insufficient time to fit in an extra activity, even if they know it would benefit them, and that they know they will give up after a short burst of enthusiasm. When they cannot get past this obstacle, and are just being self-damning because of it, I will often tell them about introducing meditation as a daily practice.

Finding time for something

I had the same problem: knew it would benefit me, knew I would not maintain it. I had even tried and experienced the burst of enthusiasm then 'sudden death' syndrome which just makes you feel worse about yourself than if you do not try at all! Eventually I started asking people who meditated regularly how they had trained themselves into the habit. Lots had used methods which would not work for me, others had more time to spare than me anyway, but then one person asked me what I meant by 'meditation'. I saw it as an uninterrupted forty-five minutes a day spent sitting still and concentrating on emptying my mind. He proposed that I found out about other meditative techniques and widened my choices. He also questioned my certainty on the time required. By making me think about my assumptions, he encouraged me to consider other ways of bringing this benefit into my life. It is now automatic for me to meditate daily . . .

Although people like to know 'the answer' I found to get the result, it is not the important part of the story. What matters about the story is that it shows that I understand the feelings of not being able to fit something in, and then it illustrates an approach to finding a way past my internal obstacle.

When someone is unaware

Because the counsellor is paying full attention to the person being counselled, they can give feedback to the individual about what they notice. This is very useful information, because the individual is likely to be caught up in what they are saying rather than what underlies it.

The unconscious response

People often do not realize consciously what their own response or reaction is to what they are talking about. The counsellor can notice the way their body language supports or contradicts their statement, and give them that information, so that they are conscious of what really matters to them, or what the effect of something is for them.

I will draw people's attention to the fact that their unconscious response is far more wholehearted towards one of their alternative strategies than others—they usually move physically in some way, and their voice tone changes. On the other hand, when people are coming up with the answers they think they should give, but are not really committed to, they will tend to say them in a neutral or flat tone of voice, and make little movement.

The counsellor may also notice things like someone saying that something is trivial, yet looking like someone to whom it matters, and vice versa. Rather than assuming that they have guessed right, the counsellor can just draw the individual's attention to the mismatch between words and body language, and ask what that is about.

The important line Often people say something without realizing what they have said. Because they are busy talking, they do not realize the import of their own words. Examples of phrases like this are: 'What I *really* want is ...' or 'If I could just ... then ...'

When people feel comfortable and safe in explaining their own thought processes, their unconscious wisdom often sneaks out and says what will really make a difference to them, but they are so caught up in their conscious thinking that they do not notice.

The counsellor can simply intervene and say, 'Did you notice what you just said?' and repeat it back to them. I find that people are often surprised, because they really did not notice, and welcome the chance to shift their conscious thinking, where it was not helping them.

Reviewing the process It is also useful sometimes to stop and just review where the individual has come to in their thinking. This type of feedback from the counsellor will help the person to notice what progress they have made, and often give them a chance to pursue a particular line further from which they had been distracted earlier in the process.

By drawing an individual's attention to what they have covered so far, the counsellor will help them to be aware of the process as well as to work out what else they need to consider.

This review is most effective if the counsellor uses an individual's own words to summarize rather than translating into the counsellor's own way of expressing things. For example, if someone has started by saying they were fed up about something, I would not say: 'You started by saying you were depressed by ...'—I would say: 'You started by saying you were fed up about ...'.

Being the other party Another way in which the counsellor can usefully intervene is by giving the individual feedback about how someone else might feel.

The individual may not be aware of the effect they have on others through body language or voice tone, and so see it as entirely the other person's problem. They fail to recognize that they are 'setting the other person up' to react in that way. Once it is appreciated that the individual's unconscious reaction is part of the reason for getting that response, they can do something about it.

I remember a manager saying to me, 'I've told my staff they are welcome to come and talk to me any time, but of course they don't.' I gently pointed out to him that, if I were one of his staff, I wouldn't take up his offer either, because his whole manner conveyed a message of contempt for his staff, and an unwillingness to be disturbed—the opposite of what he was saying. He had not been aware of this, and so was able to consider the real message he wanted to convey, what was stopping him, and how to get round those obstacles in himself. He was delighted when, in an upward appraisal several months later, he received feedback from his staff that he had become more approachable.

By pointing out the effect that their behaviour or manner could be having, the counsellor is again giving people useful information which could help them to tackle the issue more successfully. Because the counsellor has the intention of helping people to take more control of their own destiny, most people will take this information as useful. If they react adversely to it, then the counsellor has made it clear that it is only another perspective and it is up to the individual to choose whether to accept it or not.

Giving a safe place to practise

When people have realized that their approach has adversely affected them getting the result they want, they are often unsure of what they need to do to get it right. Although strictly this type of intervention would come under coaching, the workplace counsellor can usually offer them the chance to try out a new behaviour or approach by being the other party for them, and giving them feedback about the likely effect.

This gives individuals more confidence to put their approach into action in the real situation, because they have had a chance to rehearse without the risk of having an adverse effect on the real situation. When we are wanting to behave differently with someone, we often get thrown back into our old behaviours because we are a bit unsure of our approach, and the other party expects us to be like we have always been, so 'pulls' us back to what they expect. By rehearsing, we can set ourselves up more effectively to make the change, and to ignore their expectations.

I recall an employee who wanted to change the way he reacted to his manager. As soon as he saw the manager, he would be expecting criticism, so was automatically defensive. He had decided to react as if this were someone who was supportive of him. By rehearsing this with me being the manager, I was able to point out to him where he slipped back into old behaviours so he could rectify it, and also give him a chance to practise dealing with the manager's expectations that he would be defensive and expect criticism. He then felt more prepared to put his change into action in the work environment, and had worked out strategies to help himself to maintain the new behaviour.

In this chapter I have described ways in which the counsellor can directly intervene to give direction to the process of the person being counselled. The guideline is that the counsellor is to help the person towards taking more personal responsibility. By keeping the dangers of intervention in mind, the counsellor will ensure that these interventions are useful rather than creating dependency or leading the person where the counsellor thinks they should go.

If the counsellor is clear that his or her main purpose is to empower individuals and help them to reach their own useful conclusions, and that he or she is most usefully contributing to this outcome by paying full attention to what is going on with the individuals, then interventions will be automatically held within the guidelines.

Key points

- There are dangers in giving direction in workplace counselling and people need high-level awareness of the basic skills first. Otherwise they may be being helpful to make themselves feel useful, rather than to benefit the other person's development.
- It is only appropriate to give clear direction, where it will help the person towards their own empowerment.
- Because the workplace counsellor also has other roles, he or she may be able to give factual information, or take action to help the individual in their development.
- There are useful interventions the counsellor can make:
  — To help people get out of their conscious limitations by offering counter-examples, reference experiences or relevant stories.
  — To make people aware of their unconscious response, or unconscious emphasis.
  — To help people to review where they have come to in their thinking through.
  — To help people realize the effect they are having on someone else by being the other party.
- The counsellor may also propose that someone tries out a new behaviour with them before taking it into the real situation.
- Active interventions within counselling are useful only if clearly helping the person to develop their own awareness and capabilities.

PART FOUR

Designing development programmes

Having considered the various aspects of developing workplace counselling skills, Part 4 will give you some ideas of how you can design appropriate development programmes.

It is important to place any training programme within the context of development. No one becomes a good workplace counsellor by attending a course. Without opportunities for practice in the work context, with feedback, reinforcement and support, the groundwork laid in a course may be lost. In Part 4 we will consider alternative ways of enabling managers and personnel officers to develop and integrate these skills into their working practice.

11 The elements of a training programme

In any development programme for workplace counselling, the selection of what to cover will depend on two major factors.

The development needs for the individual

Any developmental programme will ideally begin with an analysis of the individual's development needs. Although this is not yet an automatic part of the process in all organizations, it is becoming more common, and as trainer you can encourage this step, by giving a simple format to at least identify the level and extent of development that would be useful.

You could use the areas identified in this chapter, with a simple list of levels of development required (see example at Appendix B). This would help the individual to assess their own development needs, and enable them to feel they have some control over the development process.

Awareness-raising

If the person concerned has not already considered themselves to be a workplace counsellor, they are likely to need the opportunity to become aware of the fundamentals of being a workplace counsellor. This is usually achieved most effectively through a training programme for groups of such individuals. Further development needs can then be identified post-course, when they understand more clearly what is required of them.

Skills development

Where people already have some experience of workplace counselling, they may just require some further development in particular skills areas. Similarly, those who have had an awareness-raising training programme may identify that they now need further development in some particular areas.

If there are sizeable groupings requiring the same skills areas, then you may, as part of the development, offer some off-the-job skills training sessions, concentrating on those particular skill areas within the context of workplace counselling. This will also reinforce the whole process for people and give added confidence in the overall practice.

If the needs are more individualized, you may use coaching or modelling to help them to develop those skills.

Contextualizing Where people already have relevant skills, and simply have not put them together to use as a workplace counsellor, then a shortened version of the awareness-raising training can be used, either with a group, or to coach individuals.

Workplace application Whatever level people start at, it is vital to ensure that the development package includes some opportunities to apply what they have learnt in the real-life situation. This is not just, 'Now go and do it'. It requires the support of feedback or opportunities to review, so that they can be confident that they are able to be workplace counsellors, and the amount of such support should be geared to the needs of the individual.

Organizational needs

The second factor which will affect what you cover with a development programme will be the requirements and constraints of the organization.

We have to be realistic as trainers. We have two levels of customers— those we train and those who ask us to take on the training in the first place. And part of our professionalism is the ability to balance their often differing needs in a way which is useful to both parties.

The outcomes wanted When the organization is requesting counselling skills for managers/ personnel staff, it has some resultant change in workplace behaviour in mind. This can range across a wide scope, and we need to be sure as trainers that we clarify what exactly is expected.

It is also possible that organizational representatives may not have thought about the results they want, in which case it is important that we discuss this with them, and devise jointly some outcomes against which the programme can be evaluated.

In my experience, organizational representatives and trainers may have very differing views of what the training can achieve, and finding a jointly agreed version at an early stage gives both sides a better chance of being able to evaluate the usefulness of the programme later on.

Constraints Although the organization may want to encourage the development of its staff, there are usually some practical constraints on how much time it is felt can be allowed for training, and in terms of cost.

We need to be able to balance pragmatism with a desire to make a genuine difference. Making it clear how much can be achieved within the expressed constraints, and giving examples of the benefits which would accrue for the organization by stretching the constraints a little are important parts of the repertoire which the trainer needs.

Trainer-identified development

Sometimes the initial idea for development of workplace counselling skills will come from the trainer. He or she may notice that this type of skill would help both individuals and the organization to be more effective.

In this case, the trainer will need to sell the benefits to both groups of clients—individual staff and organizational representatives. Although independent trainers or training companies are accustomed to this approach, internal trainers also need to develop their ability to market such ideas to their customers. Parts 1 and 2 of this book give lots of ideas on the rationale for introducing a development programme on this subject.

Added value

The overall context of changing workplace and work roles also gives the basis for suggesting how development in workplace counselling gives added value.

The skills and qualities being developed through workplace counselling are applicable in a whole variety of work situations, so are not an adjunct to managerial development, but are a part of the central core.

The application of workplace counselling brings with it increased empowerment of staff, and also has the effect of making them feel valued.

The value to the organization will be more than just some more skilled managers and personnel officers, and the trainer can use this information as part of the reasoning behind introducing the development.

Balancing the development needs

Having assessed the individual and organizational needs, you can then propose a development programme which will best fit those needs. Clearly this will vary according to the results of your assessment, so no one version of what to cover can be offered.

What I have done in this book is go through what I consider to be the essential elements of workplace counselling. I will now pull together the content which provides the menu from which a development programme can be selected to provide for the needs of the specific context.

The content of a development programme

When planning what to cover, you will need to consider what emphasis you want to give to the different elements of workplace counselling, depending on the level of development you are intending to achieve. You will also need to take into account the type of development programme you are undertaking and how the needs can best be met (see Chapter 12 for more ideas on design). In this section I will offer suggestions for core content, and additional possibilities.

Why workplace counselling?

It seems to me essential to begin by putting any form of development into a wider context. In this part of the programme I would give a brief reminder of the changes in workplace practice, and in the role of managers. Then I would suggest reasons for workplace counselling being an important set of skills for managers in the twenty-first century (see Chapters 1 and 2). This gives added weight to the value of the training for the organization and its relevance to the development of the business.

This can done by talking through the changes that are occurring, whether with individuals or a group.

Additional

You may choose to go into more detail with those who have little awareness of the implications of changes that are occurring, or to offer this as a formal presentation, with OHP slides of main points. It could also be used as part of the proposal for the development programme to convince clients of the relevance to the business.

What is workplace counselling?

In this part of the programme I would give information about the distinction between professional and workplace counselling (see Chapter 4). I would also clarify the contexts in which workplace counselling can be used (see Chapter 6).

This can be done by just talking through and responding to questions, whether one-to-one or in a training programme.

Additional

If it were with a group, I would also ask them to participate in defining the distinctions and applications of workplace counselling, so that any misunderstandings could be sorted out. I may also ask them to think of examples of good practice in workplace counselling which they have experienced, either as counsellor or as person being counselled, so that they begin to relate to the subject as something they know about, rather than something alien and new.

The benefits of developing workplace counselling skills

If the participants in the development are to commit to the programme, they need to feel that it will have obvious benefits. Because we all respond differently to potential benefits—what I see as a gain may not be perceived as such by you—I ask them to identify for themselves the potential benefits of developing the skills (see Chapter 5 for more on this theme).

Additional I may also ask them to list potential benefits to their staff and to the organization, to extend their awareness of how useful the skills are in a changing organization, and to embed some of the points made in the context-setting section of the programme.

The excellent workplace counsellor By defining for themselves the excellent workplace counsellor, the participants will identify the skills and qualities which need to be developed.

I ask them to decide what excellent workplace counsellors are like, what they do, what skills they have, and what they know about.

Additional Because I want participants to develop their confidence in being able to take on this role, I will usually follow this by asking each individual to identify one or two of the listed skills and qualities which they are already good at. This gives recognition that no one is starting from scratch on developing the skills, and that everyone brings a different package of strengths to build on for the development (see Chapter 8 for more detail).

Following on from the definition of an excellent workplace counsellor, you can ask people to stop to consider what aspects of that definition they would most like to concentrate on in the development programme. This helps to fine-tune your programme, and often elicits examples of what people find difficult to handle.

Self-management In my view this is a major part of the development process, and I devote as much time as I can to it, within the programme. If people have learnt how to keep themselves resourceful and maintain their energy, then they are likely to be more effective in the actual counselling, because they will be 'on form'.

It is easy to refer this section of the programme back to the checklist of qualities and skills, and make it relevant. Having those qualities and skills is not enough—everyone has experienced the 'trained person' who does everything you should do, yet does not have the desired effect with the client. We all have a sense of the difference between 'knowing what you have to do and appear', and a person who is genuinely committed to their role. Fundamental to achieving that genuine development is the self-awareness inherent in self-management skills.

Changing beliefs The first stage of self-management is to ensure that the beliefs which are underlying the approach are useful. By identifying the useful beliefs about self and others for workplace counselling, participants can choose to remind themselves of the beliefs which will help them to be more effective (see Chapter 7 for more detail).

Additional	I would ask them to talk about evidence from their own experience that supports these beliefs, to really confirm that they are useful.
Ways of reviving energy	Reminding people of how they can revive their energy is important. Often they have only one technique which they use, and a widening of the repertoire will be useful (see Chapter 7 for more detail).
Additional	I ask them to discuss possible ways of reviving energy and even to try them out. I also stress the importance of getting the habit of reviving energy on a regular basis, so that there is not too much 'remedial' work to do, when they need to be resourceful.
Setting the mind ready	At the least, people need to be reminded that mental distraction will adversely affect their performance, and so they will find it useful to have a technique for clearing their mind. They then can give themselves a useful conscious expectation of how the session will go (see Chapter 7 for more detail).
Additional	I may explore and try out with them several techniques which will help them to achieve the mind-clearing. I will also ask them to produce a checklist of useful expectations for a counselling session, from which they can make individual selections.
Self-management as a core skill	These aspects of self-management are placed at the beginning of the development programme because I consider them to be prerequisites to any further skill development. They are also the first stages of preparation for workplace counselling. I emphasize that they are useful techniques for setting yourself up ready to undertake workplace counselling. However, they are not a 'one-off' preparatory technique. They can also be used to regain a useful state when something throws you off balance, and used with the person being counselled to help them to be in a useful state of mind for the counselling.
Other preparation for counselling	It is important to remind people that even small steps taken to make the counselling environment more conducive to the success of the session will make a difference. Often it is difficult in the workplace to arrange for an ideal counselling environment, so I ask people to identify possible ways they can improve the environment, and will add to their ideas if necessary (see Chapters 7 and 8).
Additional	If appropriate, I may spend some time reinforcing the self-management material, by discussing the right attitude and physical state of the counsellor for setting the required tone for the counselling, and asking people to practise 'getting themselves ready'.
Setting outcomes and ground rules	To give workplace counsellors confidence that they can handle the situation and have the right to define how it will work, I will cover

material on setting outcomes and establishing ground rules for the session, so that they know how to set their parameters (see Chapter 8 for details). The level to which I take this session will depend on the needs of the individuals and the time constraints.

Skills development

Without overtly identifying it, participants will already have begun the skills development for workplace counselling through the approach used in the training. They are listening to each other, sharing ideas, reminding themselves of best practice, acknowledging different points of view, and learning to adopt useful states of mind. This makes it much easier to move into specific skills development work. For this section, there are five basic skills I would cover with participants:

1 Recognizing different worlds
2 Attention
3 Rapport
4 Questioning
5 Feedback.

Recognizing difference

People need to experience the degree to which we all interpret experiences differently, and how we differ in what will work for us. Saying it is not enough to have the impact required.

I therefore give them an activity to highlight differences and ask them to celebrate discovering differences. This breaks through the habit of making judgements and assumptions on what is different about someone, as well as asking them to actively look for the differences between them.

Additional

If I feel that more awareness of this aspect is needed, I may ask them to remember times when people imposed their point of view on them and it was uncomfortable. By talking about such experiences they remind themselves of the adverse effect of judgements and assumptions (see Chapter 8 for more on this).

Giving attention

This is another area where people need a chance to practise to enhance their ability to notice the non-verbal signs and information. Practising with each other gives them a safe and relationship-enhancing chance to do so.

Asking them to notice changes as they tell each other stories from their own lives, and to feed back on changes rather than content is an effective way of achieving this. It is important to give parameters for the stories—it is easy for people to start to tell about problems they wish they had kept to themselves within this context. I usually suggest that they describe an enjoyable time in their lives, or something significant which had positive results.

It is important to ask them to comment both on what they notice when giving attention, and what it is like to be given full attention, so that they recognize its positive effects for the other party (see Chapter 8 for more information).

Additional I may explore this in more depth by asking them to notice different things in a series of activities, and by giving them the chance to pay attention as an observer of an activity instead of a participant.

Establishing and building rapport When engaging in the previous activity on giving attention, there is usually a high level of rapport established automatically. By drawing their attention to this, we can build on it with additional points to remember for establishing rapport. Rather than give complex rules and guidelines for establishing rapport, I propose that people recognize the elements that indicate rapport, such as both parties looking physically comfortable, words flowing easily between them, and silences feeling OK.

Then we can consider what helps create this rapport, looking at environmental aspects, being comfortable yourself, giving reassurance about the intention of the session, and acknowledging the human beings involved outside their present role (see Chapters 7 and 8 for more on this).

Questioning Practising useful questions both to find out information and to help people to structure their thoughts is vital. By placing this after considering differences, attention and rapport, you can use this practice also to enhance their sensitivity in those three areas.

Again, they can use themselves as 'case studies', each offering a small niggle or irritation for the other to ask questions about. I stress that the activity is to practise asking the particular questions, rather than to resolve the issue, although that may occur as a by-product. (For the particular questions, see Chapter 9.)

Additional I may also repeat this activity, with them taking the part of someone they have found difficult to deal with, while another person uses the questions, together with the other skills. This gives a chance to get another perspective on how to deal with the difficult person, as well as a further practice with the questions.

You will notice that there are a lot of possible ways of using questions as listed in Chapter 9. Where appropriate, I may spend time going through these various applications and giving practice in them through activities.

Feedback After only being allowed to use questions to be useful to the person, people want to know what they *can* say which is useful and non-judgemental. It is then worth discussing useful feedback (see Chapter 10 for more details).

Skills practice

By engaging in a series of activities to raise people's skill levels, we can prepare them for putting these skills into a counselling session in a safe way. It is vital to remember that these are not trainee professional counsellors—they are managers and personnel officers who will also engage in workplace counselling.

We want to build their confidence in using simple skills and qualities, to help their staff to be more empowered and feel more valued. By reflecting this in the way we set up the activities we can help them to avoid the danger of trying to be professional counsellors.

I ask them to practise each of the skills separately, using their own examples of situations for the practice. Putting all the skills together only comes towards the end of the training, by which time they have gradually built up their confidence.

The structure of a counselling process

Only at this stage will I introduce the full, structured process of counselling. This is where we put together the different elements which we have examined, and look at how they can be applied to workplace counselling.

I give a handout and talk through the various stages, showing how the skills and qualities we have been developing fit in at each stage (see Appendix C for an example of a handout on the process of counselling).

Practising with the structure

This structure can be used to practise applying all the different elements of counselling which we have considered. The case studies used can be taken most effectively from the group's own experience. You can give them the various applications of workplace counselling (see Chapter 6) and then ask them to identify specifics they would like to try out.

Many trainers use video at this stage. I prefer to use 'imaginary video' as I find that people feel safer with that. I have one person being the counsellor, one being counselled, and one or two active observers. I ask them to treat the case study as a rehearsal, where they are experimenting with how to do it well. There is an imaginary pause button which anyone can press, when they have a better or different way of tackling something. They can then 'rewind' to the point where it started to drift, and 'retake' the scene trying out the different approach.

The 'counsellor' is thus relieved of the pressure of trying to do it right, and becomes the person who is acting out the different ideas. The activity then becomes a very powerful learning tool rather than a test of people's ability.

Dealing with specific issues

A final stage in the programme is to pick up on specific problems which the participants want to consider. These may be ones which they raised at the start, or ones which have occurred as they went through the programme, for example, dealing with someone who is stuck in their thinking, or unsure where to refer people. You may choose to discuss them, ask them to discuss them, or use them to prompt further sessions.

In this section of what to cover, I have offered the bare bones of a development programme. The extent to which you choose to cover any of these elements, and the methods you use will depend on the development needs, your own preferences as a trainer, and the time available. I have referred to other parts of the book, because it is designed to offer you information and ideas to support the development of useful training programmes. There are various sections I have not referred back to specifically which can be used to develop particular aspects if that is appropriate, although they would probably not appear in a basic training programme.

Key points

- Selecting what to cover depends on the individual and organizational needs. Individual needs may include awareness-raising, specific skills development, contextualizing of skills, and practice in workplace application.
- Organizational needs include both the required practical outcomes and the possible constraints.
- If the development is identified by the trainer, he or she needs to develop a rationale which meets perceived individual and organizational development needs.
- The content of a development programme should include the following:
  — Why workplace counselling? The rationale and context.
  — What is workplace counselling? Definitions and distinctions.
  — The benefits of workplace counselling: organizational and individual.
  — The excellent workplace counsellor: definition and clarification.
  — The skills of self-management: changing beliefs, reviving energy, setting the mind ready.
  — Other preparation for counselling: environment, setting outcomes, and ground rules.
  — Skills development for counselling: recognizing difference, giving attention, establishing rapport.
  — Skills development for counselling: use of questions, feedback.
  — The structure of a counselling process: practising the skills in context.
  — Dealing with specific issues.
  — Some areas may require more development than others, depending on the starting point of individuals.

12 Training programme design

In the last chapter, we considered the potential content for a development programme on workplace counselling. When designing a specific programme there are a number of factors you need to consider.

I have already raised the question of gearing the programme to both organizational and individual needs. This will affect the duration, and emphasis of content which you decide is appropriate. You can then begin to consider how you will convey the messages you wish to convey most effectively.

In this chapter we will consider some of the factors which concern effectively conveying the message.

A practical approach

The intention in workplace counselling training is to make a positive difference to the work practice of managers and personnel officers. It is therefore vital that any training and development has a strong practical rather than theoretical bias.

As trainers we need to ensure that we are well informed about the background to workplace counselling, and are clear about the principles behind it. However, this information is used to enable us to convey those principles in the way that we set up the learning of the practical skills, rather than to enable us to give a lecture on the subject.

Activities

The more we can give opportunities to practise using the skills the better. To make these activities particularly effective, we will structure them so as to make them successes rather than opportunities to fail. By doing this we build the confidence of those participating and enable them to develop from strength rather than worry about weakness. There are several ways you can design your activities to increase confidence.

Small steps

By giving them activities which only require that they try out one particular skill, you can build up to the complete application gradually.

For example, I may ask them to establish rapport within a group of three who do not normally work together—with no requirement to solve problems or discuss issues.

Not role play Wherever possible, I ask them to deal with real and immediate situations rather than role play. Many people are put off by having to take on a character, and I want to remove this barrier if I can.

For example, I may ask them to practise the useful questions with each other on a genuine niggle, so that they are being themselves. It does not matter what sort of a niggle it is—work related or home based.

Real case studies When you do want them to use a counselling situation case study, they will get far more out of using one which is real for them, rather than a hypothetical one. If I do think it would be useful for them to take on a role, for example when putting together the process of a counselling session, I find that they do so more easily when it is someone they have had to deal with.

In my experience there are plenty of real-life case studies to use from within the group, and they bring the programme directly into the work context, as opposed to being about something only distantly related.

Activities for learning By putting the emphasis on 'see what you can learn from this' when setting up activities, you relieve the pressure of trying to get it right. I use words like: 'try this out', 'explore what happens', 'notice the differences' when asking them to do an activity.

In the feedback post-activity, I ask people what they have learnt from things that worked, and then what they have learnt from things that did not work. This gives equal usefulness for learning to 'getting it right' and 'getting it wrong'. In fact, often the 'getting it wrong' can be more useful, when there is no sense of failure, only of chances to develop.

Dealing with constraints It is important to remember that these people have many different responsibilities and workplace counselling will only be a part of what they do. We may have an ideal of how workplace counselling should happen, but we must ensure that our training offers participants an achievable version of workplace counselling.

Recognizing constraints By checking out beforehand, we can ensure that our ideas are feasible within their work context. For example, we can find out if there are appropriate physical spaces for counselling or if they will have to make do with what is available. We can also ascertain what proportion of their work is likely to involve workplace counselling, and how much time they will be able to give to both the preparation and the actual sessions.

This enables us to gear our suggestions accordingly, and to give overt recognition to these constraints within the training.

Stretching constraints At the same time as recognizing the genuine constraints, it is important that we encourage people to look beyond their immediate assumptions about workplace limitations. For example, I have had a group of managers identify how they could quite easily create a 'counselling space', once they realized that it would help them to be more effective. The problem of not enough time can also be reduced when they are convinced that time spent on preparing for and effectively carrying out workplace counselling can save the time spent on recurring problems.

Recognition of experience

To encourage people to develop the required skills and abilities, it is always good practice to recognize the experience they already have which can provide a foundation for development.

We have already considered how to give initial recognition by checking out their training needs, and starting the process of development from the right level. There are other ways we can give this recognition within the programme.

Using their examples

The point made earlier about using their examples as case studies can be extended into using their examples of good practice as well. By giving an example yourself of when you noticed a mismatch between body language and the words being said, and then asking for examples from them of the same sort of thing, you are encouraging them to remember personal experience of good practice.

Newcomers to counselling

Even if people believe they have no experience of workplace counselling, it is possible and useful to draw on their life experience. Firstly, they will usually have examples of applying the approach, even if they did not call it counselling, with friends or relatives if not at work.

Secondly, they will usually have experienced someone using the approach with them. Again, it may not have been called counselling, and it may have been outside the work environment, for example a teacher helping them to sort out what career they wanted to follow, or a friend helping them to sort out what to do about a personal relationship.

Accepting their opinions

When people say that something wouldn't work for them, or that they know that you *can* do something effectively which you believe wouldn't work, it is important to accept and work with that perspective.

I find it useful to remember that everyone has valid experience and will have a slightly different way of making things work for them. There are several ways of handling these differences:

- Agree that a variety of strategies are needed to cater for different situations and ask them to extend the possibilities further.
- Accept that something may not work, and propose a different approach, or ask for their ideas.

- Accept that something you do not believe to be effective could work, and define the circumstances which would enable it to be effective with the person making the problem.

By respecting their opinions we validate their experience and can then build on it.

The value of experience

By drawing on their own experience, people can relate the subject to their own world, and make the transfer of learning much easier. It also increases their confidence in dealing with workplace counselling as something they already have some knowledge of. And, of course, it is giving value to individuals in the same way as we wish them to value those they counsel.

Setting the tone

Within the approach to workplace counselling we are developing, we give emphasis to the difference it makes if you set the right tone. It is therefore particularly important that we practise what we are preaching in the way we set up this training.

Valuing the participants' perspective

The points made in the section above about valuing the experience and opinions of participants is one of the ways in which we demonstrate that we value their perspective. If we give plenty of opportunities for them to contribute ideas and suggestions and treat everything they offer to the discussion with respect and consideration we will confirm this.

In my experience, people respond very quickly to this approach, firstly by not making deliberately cynical or negative suggestions, and secondly by being prepared to share ideas even if they are not sure they are perfectly thought through.

Space for individual needs

If we cater for individual differences, people will feel more comfortable in the training, and be able to relax and get more out of it, as well as feeling respected. Examples may be allowing someone to opt out of an activity, or as simple as giving permission to get a drink when someone wants to, rather than wait for official breaks.

If someone raises a specific issue which obviously matters to them then to deal with that on the spot, or to return to it and refer directly to it at the appropriate point in the programme, is another indication that you are treating the person with respect.

Empowerment

I have stressed the importance of involving the participants, and valuing their contributions and experience. These should be intrinsic to programme design and are all part of the empowerment process.

Our role is to facilitate participants' development so that they feel able to take on workplace counselling. The more ways we can enable them to feel in control of this development the better.

One obvious way of doing this is to consider the information you want to convey to them, and see how often you could structure an activity to elicit the information from their shared wisdom, rather than tell them.

Safety It is imperative that people feel safe in the training environment, and it is up to us to set up that safety. We need to clarify ground rules with our participants, just as we suggest to them that they do with people they are counselling. People will talk about personal things, and explore personal skills and qualities more openly if they know that it is safe to do so.

Ways of making it safe It is imperative that there is agreement that issues discussed within the training are not general knowledge to be used outside. You can add to the feeling of an implicit safety by holding training events away from the normal workplace. This makes people feel more relaxed and takes them away from their normal roles. You can also make the environment as comfortable and informal as possible. Just removing tables, bringing in a bunch of flowers and so on can change the tone.

Finally, you can ensure that activities are structured to allow people to experiment and explore, rather than try to get it right. I often add to this by giving examples of my own not so skilful attempts at these activities, to make the point that we all mess it up sometimes, and can gain learning from that if we do not chastise ourselves for it.

Planning the programme

When you are deciding what exactly you will do in the programme, you can enhance significantly its effectiveness if you create a menu rather than a set programme. By having prepared a repertoire of possibilities, you are able to respond to specific needs and demonstrate the flexibility and responsiveness we wish the counsellor to have.

Core programme To plan in this way, you need to decide which are the essential elements of the development programme. They may need to be taken in a particular order, and it is worth checking your assumptions on that, as the order can often be changed round to respond to the group's or individual's needs.

When you have identified the essential elements, it is worth considering alternative approaches to covering each of these items. With one group, a five minute input may be enough. With another, asking them to work in small groups on their ideas on the subject, and then adding to their feedback may be more effective.

The extras   Each of the essential elements may have possible spin-offs on particulars. This includes additional ways of covering the element—you may want to give more emphasis to the learning because it is an area people are unsure of.

The spin-offs may also be ways of dealing with other related issues. For example, when considering setting parameters, you may choose to explore how to create a referral reference list.

By having a menu of material prepared, you can offer a flexible programme which meets the needs of the trainee counsellors more effectively.

Variety of approach

When planning your programme material, it is important to consider how you can vary the methods you use to enable development. You need both to cater for differing needs in those you are working with and to offer a programme which is designed to facilitate learning. By asking yourself how you can vary the approach, you can develop a range of methods for conveying the message you want to get across, and then select those which will be most useful to the group or individual.

It also means that you can build in approaches which are designed to increase skills without overtly saying so. For example, I ask people to work in varied small groups, both in composition and in size, for different activities. This enhances their rapport and relationship-building skills, and their ability to recognize and respect differences through the process, although the activity itself may be about something totally different.

Conveying the message

Every trainer has a personal preferred style, so it is not useful to lay down specifically a training programme. However, we all need to stop sometimes and reconsider how we are conveying the message of the development to our participants. By suggesting these factors to be taken into consideration, I hope that I have offered a framework to help you to check through your design.

Key points

To enhance the effectiveness of your development programme design, you need to consider the following points:

- Make the training practical in orientation by:
  - using activities which divide learning into small steps, use people's own experience, have real-life case studies, and emphasize learning rather than getting it right;
  - recognizing and catering for organizational constraints;

- — giving value to and building on people's experience of using relevant skills and abilities.
- Set the right tone to the development programme by:
  - — valuing the participant's perspective;
  - — giving space for individual needs;
  - — empowering the individuals;
  - — setting up a safe environment where people feel relaxed and able to explore possibilities without judgement.
- Plan the programme in a flexible way by:
  - — having a core programme of essential elements;
  - — having various approaches to enabling learning of the core;
  - — having possible additional material ready to meet specific needs, as a menu;
  - — ensuring that you have a variety of methods to call on to facilitate learning.

Trainers will then design programmes in their own way, to suit their individual style.

13 Modelling

So far in Part 4, we have considered the ways in which we can enhance the planned learning and development of workplace counsellors. Yet this is not the learning which has most impact on us.

What is modelling?

Modelling is the natural and unconscious way in which we learn. It is how all children learn to fulfil their social and cultural roles initially. They watch and listen with fascination to find out how people function in the world, and then imitate what they observe, and gradually integrate it in their own unique way as a part of who they are. There is a saying in modern management culture, 'Walk the talk', which reflects the awareness that it is the model that people follow rather than the stated theory.

It is vital to be aware of the impact you have through your attitude and behaviour, and to take as much care with what you are modelling as you do with what you are saying.

The trainer as model

The most powerful message about the effectiveness of the workplace counselling approach will be conveyed through your approach as a trainer. However well you prepare your development programme, its effectiveness will be marred if you are not a living example of how the approach works.

Developing yourself as a model

We can actively enhance the model we present by consciously checking the various factors which unconsciously affect the message we convey. This starts with the beliefs we have about workplace counselling.

Conviction of its value

The first stage of being an effective model is to be genuinely convinced that developing these skills and abilities is worth while for individuals and organizations. If the trainer is not convinced of the usefulness and value of the intended development, then the material presented will lack an essential element—do you remember the difference between teachers at school who loved their subject, and those who just taught it?

In Parts 1 and 2 of this book, I presented a number of ways in which the development of workplace counsellors can be perceived to be valuable and useful, to both organizations and individuals. If you continued to read, then you are already convinced to some degree. If you need to increase your conviction, you can re-read those first chapters and then devise your own checklist of reasons why such development is worth while.

Conviction of its feasibility

The second area where you need to examine your beliefs is regarding the capability of others. You need to genuinely be convinced that it is possible for managers and personnel staff to be effective workplace counsellors. Again, remember the difference between how you respond to teachers who believe you can achieve something, and those who have doubts about your capability.

> It was the absolute certainty of my initial teacher of Tai Chi that anyone could learn this graceful movement that brought me past my feelings of clumsiness and tempted me to try it out. He laughed when I said that I thought I would not be able to do it, and simply suggested that I attend one session and see. He managed to inspire all of us to become more flowing and graceful in our movements, as well as encouraging us to laugh when we did not get it right, then to try again. This gentle approach led me to join a class, and become a lifelong 'addict' of Tai Chi.

Again, throughout this book, I have implicitly proposed that workplace counselling involves skills and qualities that most people already have to some degree. Our work as trainers is to help them to bring these skills and qualities out more, and combine them in the package which constitutes workplace counselling.

To enhance your conviction, you can collect evidence for yourself. Spend time in a workplace setting and notice how the counselling skills and qualities are being used, albeit unconsciously, by people there. Notice how people deal with their friends, their relatives when they are 'on form'.

By increasing your own evidence that it is possible to become an effective workplace counsellor, that most people do have some degree of the skills and qualities, you not only convince yourself, you also have more information to convince the people who come to the training doubting their own ability.

Congruency with the message

Your genuine conviction that effective workplace counselling has value for the counsellor, the person being counselled and for the organization, and that the majority of those who come forward for the development will be capable of becoming effective workplace counsellors will have a significant positive effect on the impact of your development work.

The underlying messages you will automatically convey will be that it is worth while and that people can do it. These messages are unconsciously picked up by those you are working with, and affect their attitude towards the development.

This is also a way of modelling the importance of attitudes and beliefs in the workplace counsellor. They, too, need to believe that they are doing something worth while, and that people being counselled are capable of developing their own potential.

Unconsciously, people will pick up this congruency with the message at both levels. Another way of adding to that congruence is by matching your approach with your trainees to the approach you want them to develop with those they will counsel.

Being respectful

The word respect has originally a combination of meanings: to see behind the façade, to value, and to be considerate towards. It is this combination of meanings which we wish to convey as being the way to approach others. As one of my teachers asked: 'Do you want me to be polite, or would you prefer me to respect you?' Politeness is a superficial level of respect, without depth or real meaning. True respect for another accepts that they are different and the validity of the differences. It also challenges people to be the best they are, rather than taking the presented version of who and what they are.

If we want our trainee counsellors to approach the people they counsel in this way, then it is crucial that we use this approach with them. They then experience the positive impact the approach has on the other party for themselves, and recognize experientially its value. They also have live examples of how to be respectful through your demonstration.

As trainers we need constantly to model paying full attention, respecting differences, accepting different opinions and perspectives, and stretching people to be the best that they can be. Our approach to setting up activities, taking feedback, dealing with questions, and responding to the different individuals and their behaviour within the group will significantly affect the degree to which the trainee workplace counsellors take on this approach when they deal with others. Throughout the descriptions I have given of the approach to use in the training you will notice a built-in assumption that you are modelling best practice.

Encouraging empowerment

Another crucial example we are setting as trainers is how to be empowering for others. Traditionally, within Western culture people have not been encouraged to be empowered. We have been brought up to be victims and blamers, with low self-esteem and a feeling of not being in control of our own destiny. Despite the current prevalent usage of the word empowerment in the workplace, most people still feel disempowered, and most are more effective at creating that feeling in others, rather than encouraging their empowerment.

You have the perfect opportunity to demonstrate a different approach within a development programme, as most people will come to the training already feeling disempowered—being a learner, and having an expert teacher is a context where people experience disempowerment.

By building on, rather than ignoring their previous experience, by asking them to come up with definitions, strategies and ideas, rather than telling them the right answers, you will demonstrate how empowerment can be encouraged in others. Again, they will experience the positive effect of being empowered, as well as absorb the 'how to' which you are demonstrating.

Empowerment as a learner

Within this context, we can also encourage people to recognize learning as an empowered state, rather than a position of disadvantage. This is important in workplace counselling because most people being counselled will be learning—if they already knew consciously how to deal with the issue, they would not be there. We can model this in several ways:

1 We can encourage them to take control of their learning, by stating what they need in order to learn, by encouraging them to ask for more or a different form of clarification if required, so that we are the resource rather than the controller.
2 We can set up activities as a chance to experiment and to explore rather than as a test.
3 We can be a model of empowered learning. The trainer who can say comfortably, 'I don't know that. Let's see if we can find out', is more effective than the trainer who sees not knowing as a loss of face.

Individualized solutions

A major feature of workplace counselling is that it enables individuals to find a resolution which will work for them by helping them to structure and organize their thoughts and feelings in a useful way. If the training in workplace counselling comes across as telling people the only way to counsel, then it will contradict the basic message.

The approach to developing workplace counselling skills which I have outlined in this book gives the structure of effective workplace counselling, but allows people to customize it to suit themselves and the specific situation. For example, the emphasis is on paying full attention and responding to the cues the person gives, rather than a set of rules which says: 'If they do or say this, then you must do or say that.'

By actively encouraging people to take the basic principles and then individualize them, we model the importance of allowing the person to know what is best for them.

We also enhance this message when we encourage groups to come up with possible strategies rather than the right answer.

> For example, I may suggest that they look at ways of dealing with someone who has been forced into the counselling situation rather than chosen it. I propose that they list all the ways they can think of between them of ameliorating this situation. I then suggest that each individual can select from this the strategies which appeal to them personally.

As trainers we need to look for every opportunity to model the approach which encourages individuals to customize and own solutions rather than perceive them as an imposed rule or obligation.

Using questions   Modelling this approach also gives us a good opportunity to demonstrate how the useful questions are effective. We can use the finding out questions to ensure that we are not making assumptions when people are giving comments, or feedback. We can use the structuring questions to set up activities or to gain participation in responding to queries or issues raised by individuals. And we can use the thought into action questions to prompt participants into transferring the good ideas on the programme into the personal actions they will take in the workplace context.

Being a model of workplace counselling

When helping to develop these skills, you are not being a workplace counsellor—you are a trainer. However, many of the skills and qualities will fit within the training situation.

Remember that we learn most through observing and experiencing how it is done, not through being told what to do. The more we can model the application of these skills and qualities, and their effect on others, the more powerful our message will be.

Living the model   This responsibility as trainer of setting the example of how to practise the approach goes beyond the immediate context of the development programme. If we genuinely want to 'walk the talk', then we need to remember that *all* our behaviour has an impact on others' learning. If I am very respectful of differences within the programme, but then critical and judgemental of others during the breaks, I demonstrate that you do not have to be respectful, you only have to act as if you are in the specific context.

This is particularly important in the context of workplace counselling, where the same person may be counselling and running the team meeting. If he or she treats people with contempt in the meeting, then no one will believe that they are genuinely respected within the counselling session.

For this form of development to be truly effective, the trainer must ensure that he or she can be the message consistently and give living proof that the approach is useful and effective in dealing with others. The best feedback that you can have about your training is not that people remember what you presented, but that people saw how it worked effectively.

Explicit modelling

So far, I have emphasized the unconscious message that you convey in setting an example of applying the skills and qualities.

You can also enhance the awareness of your participants by sometimes making the modelling explicit. This can take the form of reviewing an activity, making explicit the skills and behaviours you used and asking them to remark on the effects upon them, and the results they achieved.

You may even choose to demonstrate the approach by undertaking a piece with a volunteer participant around a real issue they wish to resolve. In this instance you need to be sure that you really do embody the approach, as people will notice any mismatch immediately between what you say and what you do. You can do this type of explicit modelling on a smaller scale, regarding one aspect of the skills which you feel comfortable with, rather than put yourself 'on trial'—not a useful model for your participants!

Giving useful information as a model

Through observing the behaviour and the expression, both verbally and non-verbally, of feelings connected with it we also pick up information about the state of mind which is governing the behaviour.

> Children will express this connection that they make by saying, 'Don't be angry, Mum!' when the parent is trying very hard to control her anger, but betraying it through the forced smile, sharp tone to her words, or tension in her body!

This 'knowing what's really going on' is an awareness that we carry with us into adulthood, but have often learnt not to acknowledge. When we are learning naturally and unconsciously we pick up something of the underlying attitude as well as the behaviour.

Once we are aware as trainers that we are able to affect the learning of others by the model we provide, we can enhance its effectiveness by making explicit some of the thoughts we have which help us to automatically produce the behaviour.

'This is the type of thing I say to myself when I am about to engage in workplace counselling. These are the images I see in my mind to help me to set myself up appropriately.' Any such explicit examples will help people to learn more effectively how you set yourself up to produce the behaviour.

Modelling as an approach to development

Most of the time, learning from a model takes place without conscious awareness. As a trainer, you need to be aware of the fact that people will probably learn more from how you are and how you do what you do, than from what you tell them they should do.

Because it is so powerful as a way of learning, we can use it as a consciously chosen method to enhance people's development.

The principles of modelling

You begin by explaining to people how modelling works—although everyone is both a model and a learner from other models, most people are unaware of the process.

I usually begin by reminding people that little children do not work hard at learning the basic functional and social skills, they just 'pick them up'. This is our natural learning ability, and it is only when we are told that you have to work hard to learn things that we begin to find learning difficult.

I then spell out the elements of modelling: observing the way others set themselves up to do whatever it is, physically and mentally, and then how they are as they do it: physical positioning, voice tone, and general manner. I point out that as small children we have a limited choice of role models, but as adults we can choose models of best practice from a wider range.

Sitting next to Nellie

The age-old way of learning a job by 'sitting next to Nellie' has been decried in recent years, because people learnt all the bad habits of 'Nellie'. Yet this process continues because we automatically learn from others around us. How many people leave a training course with a determination to try something different and within a few weeks have reverted to the 'normal' practice in their work environment?

If we can make people conscious of this unconscious learning process, they can then choose who they will use as a model, and by consciously selecting to model someone, they stop the unconscious absorption of less useful models.

The process of modelling

By making explicit the process of modelling, we can offer people a method of developing particular skills or attributes which they can apply in their own way, and which does not require training courses.

Identifying the skill or attribute

The first step is to decide what exactly you want to develop. In the context of workplace counselling, it is important to clarify what will be most useful for their development. Do they want to improve a particular aspect such as their ability to be non-judgemental, or do they want to improve their ability to put the package together as workplace counselling? In the latter case, they will need to find models who are already counselling effectively in the workplace and can find a way of being comfortable with them sitting in on sessions. In the former case, they can draw on a wider selection of models from both inside and outside the workplace.

Choosing the model

When selecting the model, it is important to ensure that it is someone you have some liking for or affinity with. The choice cannot be purely rational, nor can it be imposed. If we do not have some affinity with the person, we unconsciously reject the model and do not learn well from them. What is more, the sense that we would like to use the person as our model usually indicates that they are an appropriate model for us. There is always a variety of ways of being good at something, and different ways will suit different people.

I also encourage people to choose models from as wide a range as possible for specific development. The local shopkeeper may be a more useful and more accessible model for developing rapport quickly and easily than the human resources director. There are also practical considerations, like accessibility and willingness to be a model, to take into account.

Enrolling the model

This can be undertaken with or without the conscious agreement of the models. You can just observe the information which is available to anyone about how they are, how they behave, and how they express themselves. This will give people a good start, and opens up the range of available models. For example, someone may use an interviewer on the television as a model for putting someone at ease and making them feel comfortable.

On the other hand, models who have agreed to be so can be asked for further information to increase the learning, such as what they think about, what they do to prepare themselves, and how they get in the right state.

If the model has agreed to the process, they will need to understand what it means. A simple explanation usually suffices: 'I want to get better at developing rapport with people, and I like the way you do it. I would like to be able to watch how you do it, and ask you a few questions about what happens.' Most people will say that they do not do anything special, or that it just comes naturally. This is accurate, because the part you want to model is unconscious rather than thought-out. In fact, explanations are often misleading, because the model is not conscious of the automatic things which make the most difference.

Learning from a model   Modelling involves firstly observing carefully how the models are physically before and during the practice of the ability.

- Where are they tense and where relaxed in their musculature?
- What sort of position do they adopt?
- How mobile or still are they?

Then you can observe their way of speaking:

- Is it fast or slow?
- What sort of voice tone do they use?
- Are there particular expressions or emphases they use?

If you are able to ask questions, then the useful questions are:

- What do you think about when you are getting ready to do *x* or when you are doing *x*?
- What do you picture to yourself?
- What do you say to yourself?
- What makes it important for you to do *x* well?
- What do you notice about the task/the person/the environment when you are doing *x*?

These give you an indication of the state of the models, and some of their beliefs and values which produce the behaviour. These points also are interesting for the model because they have usually not considered these things consciously before you ask. It works best if you ask the questions just after the model has actually done whatever it is, as they can then recall more easily what is usually automatic for them.

Trying on the model   Once you have collected this information, the next stage is to 'try it on'. This means adopting their physical positioning, using the same way of speaking, and saying and picturing the same or similar things to yourself. This stage is pure mimicry, and is best tried out in private. When children do this, we call it playing, and I suggest that adults 'play' as well, rather than trying it out in the real-life context. A useful analogy is the idea of ordering clothes from a mail-order catalogue, so you can try them on in the privacy of your own home, and experience what it feels like and looks like to wear them, before you make your final choice.

Customizing the model   You can now adjust the model to suit your own style, so that rather than mimicry, you begin to integrate it with your individual approach. Again, at this stage, you can experiment, until it feels comfortable and you have fine-tuned it.

Then you can start using it 'in public' and make final fine adjustments until it becomes an automatic part of how you behave and think.

The value of modelling

Modelling is one of the most powerful methods of developing our own abilities. It is consciously following the process by which we learn naturally and easily, and so becomes an easy way of learning by choice.

It also focuses our attention on how we want to be, rather than what is wrong with how we are, and what might be causing our lack of ability. This means that our energy is used in improving the situation rather than analysing the problem.

Finally, it reminds us to look for the examples of best practice and use them to help us to develop, rather than try to work it all out for ourselves and be forever re-inventing wheels.

Key points

- Modelling is the natural and unconscious way in which we learn.
- The trainer is a model for participants in development programmes for workplace counselling and needs to be conscious of what he or she is conveying:
  — You must be genuinely convinced of the value of workplace counselling.
  — You must genuinely believe that it is possible for most people to develop the requisite skills.
  — You must be a model of the skills in practice.
- In particular the approach taken throughout the training needs to be respectful, empowering, and allowing of individual differences.
- The trainer is a model within formal situations, but also in the informal contact. You therefore need to live the model.
- The example you set of 'walking the talk' will have more impact on participants than any amount of clever words.
- Explicit modelling, i.e. telling people to notice the example you are giving, can be useful.
- Modelling can be used as a method of developing the requisite skills and abilities in participants.
- By explicitly giving participants the principles and process of modelling, they use it to increase their development.
- The process of modelling:
  — Identify the skill of attribute you want to develop.
  — Choose a model.
  — Enrol the model.
  — Observe, ask questions and learn from the model.
  — Try on the model's approach.
  — Customize to integrate with your individuality.
  — Practise consciously and fine-tune until it becomes automatic.
- The values of modelling as a method:
  — It is a natural learning process.

— It focuses attention on improvement rather than the lack.
— It saves re-inventing wheels.

14 Coaching

In Chapter 13 we began considering other methods of development besides training programmes, when I proposed that modelling could be used as a way of enhancing specific skills and abilities.

There are definite advantages to some part of the development programme being implemented through training workshops with a group working together. They have the opportunity then to learn from each other, and to share wisdom and experience.

However, in some circumstances, you may find that coaching as a method of development is more appropriate:

- To support and further the learning through the training workshops.
- Where there are only one or two requiring the development.
- Where they need some more help to learn from the training.
- Where the groundwork is already laid and they need only specific pieces of the overall development.

What is coaching?

There are many excellent books on coaching and I do not propose to go into detail about the methodology or process here. I will simply highlight its usefulness in the context of developing workplace counselling skills.

Coaching is a more focused form of training where the coach works with the person to help them to develop in particular ways. It is about making ideas work effectively in practice. It requires of the coach two skill-sets: a breadth of experience and knowledge regarding the subject matter; and an awareness of how to enable learning in others.

Experience

To be a useful coach, you need experience of putting into practice the principles which you are encouraging people to take on, and of using the skills and abilities which you are helping them to develop.

Trainers may have this experience from helping people to identify their development needs, and also because people often use trainers to seek help about specific workplace issues they have, as the trainer is seen as being detached from the situation yet aware of the context. Sometimes the trainer may not use this as an opportunity to apply workplace counselling skills, but instead give direct advice. None the less the potential is there for using this approach.

Someone who is perceived to be an experienced workplace counsellor may seem to be the obvious choice as coach. This may be a manager who has already developed the requisite principles and skills and is practising them on a regular basis. It is important to ensure that this coach also has the second skill-set.

Awareness of how to enable learning in others

A coach is more than a model. The manager may be an experienced workplace counsellor, and may be able to model the skills and attributes in practice, and yet still fail to coach successfully.

The coach helps people being coached to structure their learning process, and actively adds to the learning. So he or she needs to recognize how to enable others to learn and how to use and convey their experience in a way which adds to the learning. If, then, you choose to use experienced workplace counsellors as coaches, it is vital that they develop their coaching skills.

The trainer should already have developed this skill-set, and needs only to consider where it is appropriate to use coaching as a means of development.

Coaching within training programmes

When conducting training programmes on workplace counselling, the trainer's role is primarily to structure the process in order to facilitate learning. However, there are points at which he or she can add significantly to the learning by coaching individuals and even whole groups.

Examples of best practice

When dealing with a topic like workplace counselling, there are no clearly defined and accepted models of good practice—you cannot offer the group an exemplar as you can in report-writing, and say 'this is what we're aiming to achieve'. The use of the word counselling adds to the confusion—it is still linked in most people's minds to the professional counsellor (see Chapter 4 for more on this).

The trainer therefore needs to coach people into some understanding of what is meant by a workplace counsellor, so that they have some framework for developing criteria and standards. You can just give information, but it seems to me that we can coach more usefully by offering people examples of best practice to give the frame, and then allow them to take that lead and use it to develop their own ideas.

You will notice that I often suggest you give examples, which will help people to recognize what the skills and qualities of a workplace counsellor are. Although you may sometimes be able to refer to an example from within the workplace, I find that 'everyday' examples are more useful, as they are ones which everyone can relate to: the excellent doctor, the local shopkeeper, the close friend.

I find that it is helpful to offer contrasting examples: the friend who insisted on telling me what to do, and the friend who helped me to sort out what I wanted to do. Using personalized examples—'This is my experience of the approach used well'—makes them more real, and encourages people to think through their own experience.

Coaching by demonstration

Sometimes it is appropriate to offer a live example of good practice by demonstrating how to apply the particular skills yourself.

I believe that it goes against the principles of the approach we are using to put participants on the spot. Having a participant demonstrate their skills in front of the group, when they are still learning, is putting them in a very unsafe position, since people will identify the weaknesses publicly. Knowing this, the participant is likely to be anxious and not give of their best, thus receiving even more negative feedback.

On the other hand, if you demonstrate the skill, you can show the group how you want them to use it, rather than how you do not want it to turn out. You can also give them the opportunity to observe the effect on the person being counselled of good practice in applying the skills.

I use this type of coaching particularly where I am asking them to do something different from their usual approach with others, such as the use of questions to help someone to resolve their issues.

Coaching by intervention

When the participants are engaged in activities in small groups, the trainer has a good opportunity to offer useful coaching. As you go around the groups and observe what is happening, you can step in and help them to learn more through the activities.

Where the instructions for the activity have obviously not been clearly grasped, I will step in and clarify again, taking full responsibility for the misunderstanding—my lack of clarity rather than their failure to understand. Often I will give a short demonstration of how it works, to help with the clarification.

Where the group has become 'stuck' in an activity, I will intervene with suggestions of how they might get going again, by offering ideas for taking a different perspective, a different approach, or even that they step away from it and refresh themselves, so that they are in a better state to have another go.

When the groups are producing checklists or strategies, and I notice that some I consider important are missing, I may prompt them by asking questions to broaden their view. I may even join a group, and add in some ideas myself.

Coaching each other Where you have a group of people working together, you can encourage them to offer each other coaching, as a way of constructively using experience or insights to help each other.

I point out to them that they are in an environment where they can significantly enhance each other's learning by giving feedback which would not normally be given explicitly in the real-life situation. Most of the time, we are not told if what we are doing is not working well—we just have the negative results! And it is very rare for people to proactively suggest to us how we could deal with them more effectively—we usually just have to try things and hope!

Giving feedback To ensure that the feedback that participants give to each other is useful coaching, you need to offer them some structure to the feedback.

> I use this as a simple instruction:
>
> Tell others what they have done well. Describe it specifically and describe its effect on the other party. (I then give an example of what they might say.)
>
> If you notice that something they are doing is not working, stop them and tell them. Point out its effect on the other party, and suggest an alternative approach that they could try out. (Again, I give an example of what they might say.)

I point out that it is more useful to stop someone when what they are doing is not working than to leave them until they get completely stuck, by which time they will have become disheartened. If the 'coach' cannot think of an alternative approach, then he or she should still intervene, and say that they do not know what else might work. This gives both a chance to stop and explore possibilities, and learn together.

I make clear that the purpose of this type of feedback is to give both the 'coach' and the person being coached an extra source of learning. The 'coach' learns by noticing what someone else is doing well, as well as being able to suggest alternatives and see how they work. The person being coached learns by someone else helping them to become aware of what they do when something works—we are often unconscious of what made the difference—and having someone else help with ideas of what might work when they are stuck.

Being the coach I propose that people coach when they are in the role of observer, because they can then notice what is happening in a useful way. I also propose that they coach when they are the person being counselled.

They often have insights about this person's feelings and reactions which we would not normally find out about explicitly.

There is also useful learning for the coach in these two positions. It helps them to understand how others are reacting to them as counsellor, when they can observe how someone is reacting to another person who is being the counsellor. In the position of the person being counselled, they add to their awareness of how what they do affects the other person. (For an example of how to use this process, see the description of the activity for putting all the skills together in Chapter 11.)

Coaching individuals Often, with a training programme, we can usefully offer individualized coaching to enable someone to develop some particular skill, or to help with a specific issue. This may occur within the context of an activity, or it may be that we take 'time out' with that individual. For example, someone may have expressed doubts about their ability to clarify outcomes with the person being counselled. I may choose to be their partner in the activity on clarifying outcomes, so that I can coach them within the activity.

Alternatively, I may take the opportunity of everyone else being engaged in activities, or a break time, to offer some individual coaching so that they feel able to take part in the main activity on the subject.

Sometimes, with the permission of the individual, I will take that issue and coach the whole group on it, either using them, or some other volunteer, to help me. Often an individual is expressing a concern that could well be shared by others in the group, and I always commend them for daring to voice something that will be an issue for others as well.

Coaching as the main method of development

There are two contexts where coaching may be the main method of development:

- Where they only need specific pieces of development.
- Where there are too few involved to put together an initial training programme.

Specific development When people only need to develop specific aspects of their workplace counselling skills, it may be more appropriate to offer individual coaching. Many of the techniques and suggestions I have made with reference to training programmes can be easily adapted to the one-to-one situation. You can be the other person for them to practise with, you can still give them examples, information and tasks to do, and you can sit and discuss the results with them.

You can also coach them on the job, observing their practice and then helping them to review it and learn from it. It is important to remember that this is a very intense form of learning, totally focused on the individual. We need to ensure that they remain in a resourceful state, and that we pace the development programme in a way which suits them.

Small numbers When using coaching as a method to develop basic awareness and skills, because numbers are too few for a training programme, it is important to remember that they are missing the support and safety of the group, and the opportunities to work together and share ideas.

Where there is more than one, I will tend to bring them together for some parts of the development programme, so that they have some opportunities to share ideas and practise together.

Again, the programme of coaching needs to be paced differently to a training programme—the focus on the individual is much more intense, and they need space to absorb each stage of the coaching.

We also need to ensure that those being coached are not rushed into on-the-job coaching. They need to be able to explore ideas, principles and skills before they are expected to put them into practice.

Planning the coaching The advantage of coaching as a method of development is that it can be perfectly tailored to suit the needs of the individual. With a training programme, you are bound to have to generalize to some extent, to deal with differing needs within the group. With an individual, you can fine-tune and adjust your programme to support their development fully.

Initial planning While you still have the essential elements as a basic plan for the coaching, you can make adjustments in emphasis according to your analysis with the individual of their development needs. You can also discuss with individuals appropriate timing of the coaching sessions, to match with their learning pace and the other demands on their time.

Reviewing As coaching involves breaking down the development package into smaller chunks, you can review each stage of the process with the individual, and revise the development package in the light of that review to constantly fine-tune to their needs.

Making coaching effective Remember that coaching is a very focused form of development. Working with individuals requires that you develop a strong working relationship, and involve them fully in the learning process.

They are losing out on the interaction with their peers, which is a valuable part of the learning process, so there is extra responsibility on you as coach to offer support, safety, and the sense that they are not the only one who cannot grasp something.

I find that it is very useful to remind myself of some of my own clumsy attempts at counselling others, and to use these stories to reassure the person I am coaching that they are not a 'failure', but only a learner.

Coaching to support and further the learning on training programmes

If we really want to make our development programme for workplace counsellors effective, then coaching on-the-job as follow-up to a training programme is essential. Coaching is not yet generally accepted as an essential follow-up element of any development programme, despite the fact that there is a body of evidence that people would apply far more of their learning off-the-job if they were given coaching in overcoming the obstacles they meet when they try to put the learning into practice in the workplace.

Coaching on-the-job

By observing people as they try out the counselling skills in practice, and then reviewing with them what worked well and what else they could do, you can help them to refine their application of the counselling approach, and really confirm the practice.

Sometimes this process is primarily support and reinforcement. Most people, however, will benefit from active coaching, either on a specific area of practice, or on the overall application of the process.

Implementing the coaching

You can select with the person appropriate situations for observation—there are many areas of workplace counselling where the subject matter is not so sensitive as to preclude a sympathetic observer.

It is also important to gain agreement from the individual being counselled to your presence, and to clarify with them that the ground rules apply equally to you.

Coaching off-the-job

Sometimes it may be appropriate to coach individually after the training programme in a specific aspect of development.

This enables you to customize the development to suit the individual needs, where you were unable to do so within the context of the group training. For example, people may want to practise using the approach with someone who has been bereaved, because they know they will have that situation to deal with, and they are not yet confident of their ability to handle it. You can role-play such a situation with them, and coach them on their approach, so that they feel more able to handle it when it occurs.

Coaching as a developmental process

Coaching is an important tool in the development programme for workplace counselling. While I would not recommend it as the only method for developing an individual's skills, it has an important part to play in the overall process.

People learn quickly when they practise, and then review and receive constructive feedback on their practice. People learn more when they have their attention drawn to particular aspects of the potential learning. People can contribute more effectively to their own development when they are given a framework of best practice for their learning. All these are areas where coaching can give added value.

Key points

- Coaching is focused training to help someone practise the skills effectively.
- Effective coaches have both experience of applying the skills and awareness of how to enable learning in others.
- Coaching can be usefully applied within the context of training programmes:
  - To increase understanding of the requirements by giving examples of best practice, or by demonstrating the application of the skills.
  - To help clarify misunderstandings, or make activities useful, by intervening in activities to give additional information or examples.
  - To enhance learning, by giving participants the coaching role with each other.
  - To help individuals to deal with specific issues, by taking time out to offer specific coaching.
- Coaching may be the main method of development for specific skills development. It may also of necessity be used for basic development because of low numbers.
- It is vital to remember that this is a very intense form of development and requires careful pacing to suit the learning style of the individual.
- Individual coaching gives an opportunity to customize the package to suit the individual's development needs perfectly.
- Coaching should be regarded as an essential part of the follow-up to any training programme, to help individuals to fully realize their potential development in practice.

PART FIVE

Supporting the development

The final part considers the different ways in which we can support the development of workplace counselling skills in practice. Without such follow-up support, there is less likely to be a significant change in workplace behaviour, so it is worth our while to ensure that we have done all we can to make the support available.

15 Formal support for development

In Chapter 14 I emphasized the importance of coaching as part of the follow-up to a training programme in workplace counselling. Full development of an effective workplace counsellor is unlikely to occur as a result of a training programme, no matter how good it is. They need the opportunity to develop the skills further within the workplace by putting them into practice, and to be supported in that part of their development.

Factors which adversely affect full development

There are several ways in which this continuing development may be blocked, if it is not overtly recognized and encouraged.

Lack of time

We are expecting people to develop and bring together a set of skills to enhance their practice as workplace counsellors, while still maintaining the other functions and skill-sets which are already their responsibility. It is only too easy to 'not find the time' to consciously develop these skills, and for enthusiasm to try out ideas to get lost in the welter of other priorities that these people have in the workplace.

This is even more likely if there has not been acknowledgement in the development programme planning that the development is not finished once the training programme is completed.

Lack of encouragement

We all know the cynical reaction to someone who has been on a training programme and is full of new ideas: 'Never mind, give it a week or two and you'll get back to normal.' This reaction is discouraging, but sometimes line managers are even more forceful in their blocking of the practice of new techniques or ideas. They actively prevent the person from using new skills, and treat the whole idea of innovation in workplace practice as a threat to the 'normal' working.

Lack of confidence   Although people may have developed their confidence in their ability to practise effective counselling within the safe environment of the training programme, they may not feel so sure once they return to the pressured atmosphere of the workplace. They may postpone trying out the approach until the 'time is right' and end up losing more confidence as they get further away from the training programme.

'Failure'   Some people will go back to work and enthusiastically set about using what they have learnt. If, however, it does not work as well as they expected, or they realize that they have not perfected the skills for practical application, they may see this as 'failure' of either the training or themselves. In either case, this may be enough to put them off trying again. After all, old practices are comfortably familiar even if not particularly effective.

Factors which prevent full development of skills
- Lack of time to put into practice.
- Lack of encouragement in work situation.
- Loss of confidence once back in work environment.
- Experience of something not working, leading to fear of trying again.

Ensuring that development is supported

An effective development programme will include both recognition of the need for continuing support and development after the training programme, and methods of offering that support.

By taking responsibility for this important stage, the trainer enhances the effectiveness of his or her work in providing the basic groundwork. This results in enhanced satisfaction with the results of the development, for the trainer, the workplace counsellor, and the person commissioning the programme in the first place.

Recognition of the need for ongoing development

Before we can put in place a framework to support ongoing development, we need to gain recognition for its value, both from the organization and from those we are training. Although recognized as essential in some professions, including professional counselling, it is not common business practice. In fact, we often have to battle to even get people released for a day or two's training in basic 'soft' skills, because they are not seen as directly measurable for their contribution to the business objectives.

Recognition by the organization   If you are an internal trainer, you may be able to influence your own organization's policy on this, either directly, or through your department. Slowly, organizations are beginning to realize that training by itself is not enough to effect the changes they need, to continue to be successful.

The theme of continuous improvement is very popular, yet seems to be primarily applied to processes rather than management or people skills. It none the less provides an opportunity to propose that the same theme could be applied to the development of such skills as workplace counselling.

You can also collect evidence to make a business case for the follow-up support to training. There is plenty of anecdotal evidence that it makes a significant difference to the effective use of the training, but little formalized evidence. Questionnaire surveys of those trained who had follow-up support, compared with those who simply had the training would provide some factual support for the case.

It is important to remember that your case needs to be expressed in terms of value to the business, not just stating that it is a good thing for the trainees. You also need to have a clear action plan, so that you can effectively answer questions about cost, time, resources that would be involved.

Finally, it is worth stating that sometimes the reason that the practice is not policy is because no one has suggested that it should be! Merely proposing it may be enough—there may not be a major battle to fight!

External trainers   If, like me, you are external to the organization, it is more difficult to gain recognition for this form of support from the organization.

You can similarly prepare your case to justify it to the organization. However, you may find that your proposal is blocked by budgetary considerations, if there is a limited external training budget. This recognition of cost can also inhibit external trainers in proposing a full development programme, as it may seem as if they are merely increasing their own income.

There may be internal trainers who can pick up the follow-up support and implement it at no extra cost to the organization, and it is certainly valuable to work with them on ways of making this happen. Obviously, though, they may have less commitment than you have to making the particular development programme more effective, since you 'own' the training package. Involving them in the training itself is one way of increasing the likelihood of their following through.

It is also worth bearing in mind that, while you may not get recognition of the need for follow-up support immediately, you may gradually influence the organization if you continue to suggest it as the ideal, even when it has not been accepted previously.

Recognition by the trainees   It is not difficult to get participants on a training programme of this ilk to recognize the need for follow-up development and support. In fact, sometimes the difficulty is in stopping them from identifying the problems they can see, and using them as a reason not to bother to take on the potential learning.

The issue here is whether they think it is possible to have that ongoing support for their learning. Because it is not generally considered to be part of the package, many will not expect to receive it, and will not consider it to be a feasible option.

However, it is important that we, as trainers, do ensure that they overtly recognize the need for follow-up support and reinforcement, and that we overtly endorse that it makes a significant difference to the potential gains from the training.

Choice of methods of offering support

It is not enough to recognize that ongoing support makes a difference. We also need to consider how support and reinforcement may be given. There are many possible approaches to this, and the selection made will depend on what is appropriate and feasible in the context.

Factors to take account of include:

- Organizational willingness to allow for this support.
- Practical constraints of time and cost and resources.
- Preferred options of those receiving the support.

I intend to propose what the options might be, so that you are able to select appropriately.

Development programmes

If the training is a part of the development programme, then the continuing process provides a means of supporting and reinforcing the learning. The effectiveness of the training will be evaluated, and the next stages of development will be identified from the evaluation.

This formal process will support and reinforce the learning and its application in practice, thus helping the individual and the organization to gain the optimum benefit from the training.

Use of VQs

Up until recently, there were no vocational qualifications relevant to workplace counselling. However, there are now standards and competence-based qualifications in Advice, Guidance, Counselling and Psychotherapy.

Some of the units within these qualifications are appropriate for use with workplace counsellors and would provide the framework for a development programme.

Training evaluation

Even if there is no specific development programme for workplace counselling to provide follow-up support, there may be a well-established general process of training evaluation. This could provide a means of supporting the development by reinforcing the recognition that training is fully effective only when it is usefully applied in practice. It also picks up on any further development needs.

Follow-up by line manager

The first stage of this would be the post-course follow-up with the line manager, to discuss what the individual had gained from the training and how he or she planned to use the learning in the workplace.

This discussion would then lead to continuing monitoring with the manager of how the application was progressing.

Follow-up by trainer

The trainer may also have a personal evaluation process, and follow up with the participant, both shortly after the training, and after a longer interval, to discover how useful the training has been, and if there are further development needs.

Formal support programmes

Another method of ensuring that participants are supported in the development of their practice is to include a formal support programme in the training package. Rather than arranging support in the workplace, this is a method of offering support which brings the participants off-the-job and back into the training environment.

Follow-up days

Offering follow-up days as part of the programme gives the participants an opportunity to come together again and review their practice.

The ideal package consists of a follow-up day fairly soon after the initial training, and then further review days spaced at longer intervals over a period of six months to a year.

The first day

The first day is the opportunity to reinforce what is already working in practice and give recognition to it. This encourages people to keep going, and also enables them to find out how others are faring. This group support and encouragement is very valuable.

It is also a chance to identify what has not worked or does not translate easily into practice. By identifying the practical obstacles, and considering ways of overcoming them at this early stage of practice, they will have less of an adverse effect on the development.

Subsequent days

The same pattern can be used for subsequent follow-up days: a sharing of progress, an identification of obstacles, and consideration of ways of overcoming obstacles.

Setting tasks The trainer can enhance the value of these follow-up days by giving the group specific learning tasks to undertake and report back on at the next follow-up day.

These tasks may be individualized or they may follow particular themes which seem to have general relevance. Examples might be:

- Set yourself an extra five minutes in your diary before a development review with a member of your staff, and practise setting yourself up ready for the counselling approach, using the methods we covered.
- Review two counselling sessions and identify what worked well, and what you would do differently.
- Use the counselling approach questions next time someone stops you and asks you for advice on a work-related question.
- Identify five ways in which others have demonstrated respect and sympathy with you.

You may choose to let people choose their own learning tasks. At the end of the session, ask them to identify two small things they could do to enhance their practice, and then ask them to report back at the next session.

The added value of follow-up days With follow-up days, there is an expectation that everyone will turn up and take part. This gives them the chance to keep alive the feeling of a 'safe' environment created through the training programme, and gain the support and encouragement which that provides.

They also can give strong support to each other, by giving recognition to each other's progress, by sharing their learning and practical ideas, and by sympathizing with each other's predicaments, while also contributing useful ideas to help overcome them.

Clinics This is a rather different approach to including formal support in the programme. When you offer follow-up clinics, you offer a timetabled slot for people to come back and ask for help, advice, or further information. They choose whether to come or not, and the trainer deals with their specific issues with them.

This approach will only work if people are comfortable in using such a service, and the company ethos is supportive of the approach.

Clinics are particularly useful as immediate follow-up support. If there are several slots in the first few weeks after the training, then problem areas can be immediately dealt with so that they do not block the individual's development.

Mentoring Mentoring as a form of support and development is becoming more widespread in its use in the workplace. In professional counselling it is regarded as essential, although slightly differently labelled (as supervision) and defined. There are full descriptions of the mentoring relationship and process which would help you to develop this form of support if your organization does not already use it.

Essentially, a mentor is someone who provides support for an individual as they are developing. The mentor is ideally detached from the situation (i.e. not their own line manager) and has experience and a willingness to help the person develop. The mentor is a source of advice, a prompt to review what is happening, and provides a safe place to explore ideas.

The relationship established between mentor and mentee is very important. This cannot be an imposed relationship for either side, as the ability to relate comfortably and respectfully with each other is crucial to the process.

Selecting mentors

Effective workplace counsellors are likely to be excellent mentors, because many of the skills and qualities required of the mentor are the same as for workplace counselling. The person concerned must have a desire to be a mentor. Mentors need to be committed to offering support to others as they develop their skills. Some people will want to do so, because someone fulfilled that role for them. Others will want to do so, because they recognize that they would have benefited from it, even though they did not get it!

Setting up mentoring

The trainer will need to establish a directory of willing mentors and then actively work with the mentors and mentees to match them, set up the relationships, and structure the process they will use. This will be easier to do once you have established the precedent: many mentees will be glad to become mentors in their turn, as more people are developed as effective workplace counsellors.

The value of mentoring

Mentoring spreads the responsibility for supporting the development of workplace counsellors among a variety of people who all believe in the value of the development. You are not risking the adverse effects of a manager whose support is superficial, 'because I've got to'.

It gives the trainee workplace counsellor a strong sense of support because it has been set up for that purpose with an individual who is committed to it.

It also has value for the mentors who have the opportunity to use their experience and to review their own learning as they support the trainees in developing their skills.

Selection of formal support for development

I have given brief outlines of the various ways in which you can organize formal support for development. Choosing which to use depends very much on the context you are working in. The methods listed are not mutually exclusive. A mixture of them will provide a very powerful form of support. At the least, one of these methods should be used, to convey the message that the organization values the development of workplace counselling skills, and recognizes that their effective development will require some form of support and reinforcement.

Workplace counselling is an important part of the development of changing management practice, rather than just another skill-set. Because it is part of a fundamentally different approach to management, people will need help in building up the new practice, until it becomes the norm.

Key points

- Effective development of workplace counselling will require follow-up support as it is practised in the workplace.
- Factors which may adversely affect its development include:
  — people finding there is no time to put it into practice;
  — no encouragement to put it into practice;
  — a lack of confidence in their own ability to do it;
  — 'failure' at an early stage of practice.
- Supporting development requires firstly recognition of the importance of support by the organization.
- Trainees need to know that it is generally recognized that they will require follow-up support, and that they will receive it.
- The method(s) of formal support chosen will depend on context and preferences. Possible methods include:
  — overall development programmes;
  — a training evaluation process;
  — follow-up days;
  — clinics;
  — mentoring.
- Formal follow-up support conveys the message that the organization considers effective workplace counselling to be an important element of the business development.

16 Informal support for development

In Chapter 15, I highlighted the importance of follow-up support to the effective development of workplace counselling. I also considered ways of providing that support in a structured form.

There are two reasons for now pursuing the theme of support, but in an informal way. Firstly, the structured support is both finite and limited in its scope. It can undoubtedly make a significant difference, and yet we can increase that difference by ensuring that there is also informal support.

On the other hand, it may not be possible to arrange the formal support, for whatever reason, in which case it is vital to find some other means of helping people to reinforce and build their development of the skills.

I do not believe that follow-up support is an optional extra with workplace counselling. I believe that it is crucial to the success of the development. Professionally trained counsellors have some form of supervision and counselling themselves, as a compulsory part of their accreditation as a professional counsellor. Although not on the same intense level, workplace counsellors also need to be able to release some of the pressure caused by engaging in the counselling process, to share successes and frustrations, and to have a safe place to turn to for support. The informal system can be the most effective source of this support.

The benefits of informal support

It is a natural inclination on the part of the learner to look for ways of gaining support while developing skills. People find it easier to lose weight or learn how to swim when they are teamed up with others doing the same. We buy books on the subject, read articles, watch TV programmes, join clubs and societies. These are all types of informal support.

By encouraging this natural inclination, we enhance people's awareness of how to help themselves to develop skills and abilities—and, incidentally, how to help others do the same.

These informal methods which people tend to adopt naturally have potentially all the elements which will combine to give the strongest support:

- Peer support to maintain motivation.
- Sympathetic interest and encouragement to have another go.
- Sharing of successes and failures.
- Sharing of ideas and strategies.
- Feeding in of new/different ideas.
- Advice from others who have more experience.
- Potential for continuing support and development.
- Ready accessibility of some form of support.

Methods of informal support

Some of those you work with will automatically begin to build up their own informal supports. There are others who will benefit from the prompting and direction you can give.

The following are some of the obvious and less obvious means of gaining informal support, and can be suggested to people so that they can choose those which they find most useful.

I find that a session towards the end of the training where I ask what people need to help them to put the learning into practice after the programme will elicit the request for support, and often some of the possible methods. By adding to their list of methods, and by exploring how they can set the support system up for themselves, we can help to ensure that the informal support is there to further their practice in the workplace.

Trainer support

One means of follow-up support we can offer is support from ourselves. This can vary from being physically available if they want some support or reinforcement to being on the end of a phone at certain times.

We can also ensure that we 'happen' to be around in the workplace from time to time, and that we proactively approach them to find out how they are getting on.

Mentoring

I have already described this approach in the previous chapter, as formal support. However, it may also be possible in a less formalized way.

We can suggest to people that they consider whether there is anyone who would fulfil this role with them, whom they could approach and ask to help them in this way. I know of many such informal relationships which are very effective.

Organizational support

There may not be an overall sense of organizational support, yet there may well be pockets of support—particular managers, departments, group meetings, where the workplace counsellor could find support, and feel less isolated.

Peer support

Those who have been through the same training in the same group provide powerful reinforcement and support for each other. This can happen automatically as they come into contact with each other in the day-to-day work.

I would suggest that they take this a stage further, to ensure that they receive and give this type of support. They may set up informal gatherings at specific times—a sort of self-help group. They may exchange phone numbers, and times they are available. They may form sub-groups within different geographical work areas. By thinking about how they will ensure that they contact and support each other, they increase the likelihood of it happening.

Support from those they counsel

We often underestimate the amount of support and encouragement we can get from those we are 'helping'. If we can feel comfortable with telling them that we are learning, and practising to become more effective, most people are sympathetic and supportive. Interestingly, this is likely to enhance their respect for us rather than reduce it—most respond well to honesty, and like the model of someone being comfortable with saying 'I'm not sure I'm skilled in this yet', rather than pretending to a level of expertise which is not borne out by their practice.

They can ask everyone they deal with for feedback about the process:

- What did you find useful about my approach?
- What did you find less useful, and how would you have preferred me to handle it?

They can also ask certain people if they are willing to be 'guinea-pigs':

- Can I try out this new approach on this issue, and see how it works?

By being up-front about being at the development stage, they not only gain support, but also set a useful example for their staff. In the learning organization, everyone needs to become comfortable with being a learner, and supportive of others who are also experimenting and exploring.

People will find that if they take this approach, they may well receive unsolicited feedback as well, and this will often be negative, not because they are failing but because we all tend to notice what is wrong rather than what is right.

If I propose this approach, I like to prepare people for it, by building up their confidence to be explicitly a learner, and by getting them to think through the possible reactions and responses, and work out ways of making these as useful as possible. For example, if they tell people explicitly the type of feedback they want, they are less likely to hear only the negative.

Creating your own support network

These methods of support can all be prompted within the organization. However, it is not always possible to find the level of support you need within the immediate context.

I consider it important to broaden the scope of how we build support networks, because this gives people more awareness of how they can support themselves in developing any type of learning.

People support from outside the organization

Building a support network which goes beyond the organization is a prerequisite for those of us who work on our own. It is something that does not occur to some people within a workplace context. Encouraging them to look beyond the immediate context can often help them to begin to develop an awareness of how to actively find support for your own development, no matter what the context.

This may be peer support, mentors, 'safe' people to try out ideas with, or just like-minded people who will sympathize with and advise on times when you do not seem to be progressing.

I encourage people to consider all the possibilities:

- People in previous work contexts
- Relatives
- Friends
- People you have met on other courses/seminars
- People you have made contact with when finding out about referral agencies.

I also remind them that the person need not necessarily be a workplace counsellor to be a useful part of their support network. The person may be someone who has some of the skills, they may just be a sympathetic listener, or someone who enjoys encouraging others to develop, or someone with whom people feel safe in being a learner.

We then talk through ways they can enrol people as support: how to approach them; what to ask for; and what to tell them.

Support from other sources

Support networks need not consist solely of people you can contact. There are many forms of support and reinforcement which can be immediately available to us whenever we need them.

There are books, audio tapes, and videos which can offer useful support and help when someone is developing a practice. They may be material directly related to developing workplace counselling skills, or they may be to help keep motivation for development high, or they may help someone to regain a positive state when feeling that they are 'failing'.

Many trainers compile lists of additional sources of information. These can often be used by those who have a real desire to extend their knowledge, but not be used by the majority. By designing your list to inform them about how they can use the material to support their development, you can enhance its usefulness significantly. It will also, of course, have some additional material on it, which will be less directly related to the specific subject, and more on the themes of how to motivate yourself to keep developing, or how to keep yourself in a good state.

Self-generated support and reinforcement

Most of us respond well to triggers we have devised for ourselves to remind us of things. A simple example would be the photographs we take on holiday. They may not be wonderfully constructed photographs, but they serve perfectly as reminders to us of moods, moments, specific places and so on.

By making our participants aware of this, we can help them to create reminders and triggers for themselves, to support and reinforce their development. These may be to encourage them to keep going, to remind them of particular things, or to inspire them with fresh ideas when they are stuck.

Reminders of the 'mood' of the programme

I find that people enjoy being in the training programme, and feel very positive about continuing to develop. If they can devise ways of reminding themselves of this feeling, it will help to keep them going back in the work context.

- There may be a key phrase which captures the essence of that mood which they could put on a sheet of paper and stick on the wall.
- There may a group photograph.
- There may be an object which reminds them and represents the mood.
- There may even be a particular song.

What matters is that they select whatever it is as their representation, and have it easily available to them.

Reminders of particular aspects

I ask people to name one or two particular things they want to remember and use when they return to the workplace. These will be different for different individuals, and the only rule is that they cannot say 'everything'!

I then ask them to think of a way they can remind themselves of what they have chosen. This is usually a word or a symbol that they can put in front of themselves, so they have the constant reminder.

Ideas for when they are stuck

When we are working on the training programme, I regularly ask them in small groups to come up with lists of different approaches they can take to particular aspects of the development or to particular issues. These lists are then collated, and sent out to participants after the course. They serve as useful reference points when they are stuck, as well as being general reminders of the programme and the constructive and creative atmosphere.

Handouts can also serve the same purpose. However, I would suggest that people own them properly, by adding their own notes, and discarding ones they do not find useful.

Caring for themselves

This is last on the list, and yet I would consider it to be the first area to consider when developing workplace counsellors.

Workplace counselling is a satisfying role to play. Most people enjoy helping others to develop and find it both fulfilling and full of learning for them as well—others are fascinating! It is also stretching and stressful for the counsellor. It takes energy and resourcefulness to fulfil this role well. It will make life easier in the longer term for managers, because it will reduce the level to which they are expected to sort things out for their staff. In the short term, however, it will be very demanding of them, because they will not immediately gain the benefits—they are cumulative—and they will be making more conscious effort to learn and develop the approach.

I emphasize the importance of being able to create a good state in yourself at the beginning of workplace counselling training—it is an essential prerequisite. I also return to the same theme at the end of a training programme, as part of their preparation to go back to the workplace and put their learning into action.

How to relieve the pressure

Everyone has their own methods of relieving stress or pressure. I remind them of the techniques we have already considered for increasing resourcefulness, as they provide ways of relieving stress as well. I propose to people that they add in a little time after a counselling session to de-stress themselves, so that the pressure does not build up. Doing something routine and unrelated, going for a short walk, talking to someone about inconsequential matters, doing a short relaxation routine, are all useful strategies.

Keeping it in perspective

By consciously letting themselves wind down, they will automatically improve their ability to maintain a useful perspective on what they are doing.

I also suggest that laughter is a good way of keeping perspective. There is usually plenty of laughter during the training and they experience again the usefulness of not taking it all too seriously.

Finally, I remind them that, while they are still developing these skills, they may find lots of reasons to condemn themselves for not getting it right. However, they need to remember that there are other areas of their work where they are extremely effective, so a 'failure' in workplace counselling is not a failure overall. By telling themselves about the things they do well, and reminding themselves that all learners are clumsy or ineffective sometimes, they can keep this in perspective.

Constructive reviewing   The last point links into the issue of reviewing the practice. When we have been made aware of all the ways in which we could improve our practice of something, we often use this increased awareness to beat ourselves up more often! We notice many more 'mistakes' because we are now consciously incompetent.

To offset this tendency, I propose to people that they adopt the habit of constructive reviewing. This is quite a simple process, which is similar to the feedback I suggest they ask for from others. It means taking a few minutes at the end of the session, or at the end of a day. Ask yourself the following questions:

1 'What have I handled well in my workplace counselling?' Replay in your mind the parts of the interaction(s) which were effective.
2 'What would I handle differently next time?' Remember the parts you would like to improve.

Instead of replaying them as they were, imagine how else you could handle it and play through the revised version in your mind—'Next time, I will . . .'.

By adopting this practice, people stop themselves from being self-critical, because they are using their mistakes as learning experiences. They also increase the likelihood of an improved performance next time, because they have already thought about ways of revising their behaviour, rather than confirmed the less useful pattern of behaviour by playing it over and over in their head.

The more ways we can encourage people to identify strategies to support them in their workplace development of their counselling skills, the more likely they are to become effective workplace counsellors. This is surely our intention in setting up the training or development programme in the first place, and so it is worth our-while as trainers spending some time on helping people to develop a raft of support mechanisms.

Key points

- Informal follow-up support is vital to the development of effective workplace counselling.
- It may also be the only form of support available to people.

- People are naturally inclined to find follow-up support when they are learning—we can encourage and build on that inclination.
- The trainer can offer follow-up support from themselves, and also give it proactively.
- People can identify an informal mentoring relationship.
- They can find sympathetic people within the organization on an informal basis.
- They can organize ways of giving each other support.
- They can gain support from those they counsel.
- They can build an informal support network from others outside the organization.
- They can use material like books and audio tapes for support and reinforcement.
- They can generate reminders to have with them in the workplace.
- They also need to be reminded to care for themselves in the process of development, to alleviate stress and maintain their development. They can devise ways of:
  — relieving stress or pressure;
  — maintaining perspective;
  — reviewing their practice constructively.
- By helping our participants to think of methods of supporting themselves in their development, we enhance the likely effectiveness of the training.

Afterword

In Chapters 15 and 16, I have put considerable emphasis on the importance of both ongoing development and ways of supporting that development.

I believe that the same two themes are as important for you as a trainer as they are for those you train. I pointed out that your approach to the training will be taken as a model by your learners, and that you need to consciously model the skills and qualities you want them to develop. You are also a model for them of how to develop. By applying the same principles of development and support to your programmes on workplace counselling, you will both model the process for them, and continually improve the effectiveness of the training you offer on this topic.

Looking after yourself

Training in workplace counselling is intensive work. To be effective, you need to ensure that you are in a resourceful state to undertake it. You also need to allow yourself 'recovery time' when you can wind down from the process. All the strategies suggested for your participants apply equally to you.

Having a support network

It is very useful to have others with whom you can talk things through, share issues, and sound out ideas, both inside and outside the organization. Although particularly valuable when you are first beginning to train in this subject, I find that this support network has also great value in keeping me on the journey of continuously developing my ideas and methods.

Equally, support from other sources, such as books and audio tapes, can help to keep us reminded of ways of developing our programmes, and reasons for doing so.

Developing your programmes

We all need to be continuously reviewing and developing our programmes to ensure that our work is as effective as it can be.

Using the material in this book

You may already have a well-developed programme for workplace counselling, in which case I hope this book will provide you with confirmations, reminders, and sometimes a different angle on something which adds to the effectiveness of what you presently deliver.

You may just be beginning to consider offering workplace counselling training, in which case you may find that there is too much in the way of information and ideas in this book, and not enough direct guidance. It is important to recognize the stage you are at in your development of programmes and then to extend from there at a pace with which you are comfortable.

I have deliberately not laid down the 'ideal' programme of training for workplace counselling because that limits the possibilities of how you may use the material in this book. I would recommend that you take one part of the book which appeals to you, and devise ways of introducing that aspect, or using that information, in your own training. You also need to adapt ideas I put forward to fit your own training style, and your own way of expressing things. For example, my style is very participative and experiential—you may prefer something which is more directive.

Finally, it is important to recognize that there are aspects of my suggestions with which you may not agree. This is not a rule book, it is an exposition of a particular proven approach to training in workplace counselling. You will select what fits with your beliefs about such training, and ignore those parts which do not fit. I make no claim to be 'right', only that I have evidence that this particular approach is useful and effective.

Reviewing development

As you engage in running training programmes on workplace counselling, I would recommend using the approach to constructive review which I described for participants in the last chapter. You may already do this with your programmes. If not, it is a useful practice with any training you undertake.

By continuously reviewing our programmes we not only benefit from the learning ourselves, we also continuously improve the effectiveness of what we can offer to those we are there to help and support.

Conclusion

When developing managers and personnel officers in workplace counselling, we are offering something more than another specific skill-set.

We are developing their ability to manage themselves in a changing work context. We are also helping them to develop their skills in relating to and empowering others, as well as their ability to offer workplace counselling. This development can benefit them in their work life, by making it easier and more satisfying, and also in their personal lives. I often receive feedback from people on the improvement in their personal relationships as a result of the training.

This is valuable work, and deserves the best we can give to it. I hope that this book will have provided the stimulus to you to engage in the work with even more enthusiasm and enjoyment.

Appendix A The skills and qualities of an excellent workplace counsellor

An excellent workplace counsellor is:

- A good listener
- Honest
- Non-threatening
- Confidential
- Trustworthy
- Adaptable
- A people person
- Approachable
- Open
- Not necessarily an expert
- In control
- Sensitive to needs
- Positive
- Objective
- Able to put themselves in your position
- Able to put people at ease
- Able to read body language
- Able to get people to talk
- Understanding of the situation.

An excellent workplace counsellor:

- Can empathize
- Establishes rapport
- Identifies helpful actions
- Makes time
- Identifies 'hot points'
- Checks their own understanding
- Listens
- Directs sometimes
- Cares/comforts

- Helps people to find their own solutions
- Communicates well
- Identifies priorities
- Uses their natural abilities
- Makes suggestions where appropriate
- Meets people at their own level
- Is able to see things in context
- Makes counselling a positive experience for the person being counselled
- Knows their limitations in dealing with different situations
- Seeks assistance where necessary
- Knows their own strengths and weaknesses
- Recaps and summarizes
- Does not get too involved to be useful.

Appendix B Levels of development required

	Awareness raising	Skills development	Contextualizing	Workplace application
Changing context				
Changing role				
What is a workplace counsellor?				
Self-management				
Setting outcomes and parameters				
Setting the tone				
Counselling skills				
Process of counselling				
Intervening in the process				
Other specific areas				

Appendix C The process of a counselling session

Planning and preparation
- Check out and resource own state.
- Decide on appropriate timing.
- Choose appropriate environment.
- Collect any information needed pre-session.
- Have to hand any resources needed for session.
- Establish the intention of session.
- Establish your outcomes for session and criteria for a successful session.
- Check own state and comfort.

Implementation
- Welcome and put at ease.
- Break the ice.
- Establish rapport.
- Talk about and agree outcomes of session.
- Establish parameters of session.
- Find out/give the presenting reason for session.
- Elicit information.
- Pay attention.
- Listen to the whole person, not just the content.
- Check that you have understood correctly.
- Give information/feedback appropriately.
- Summarize.
- Encourage identification of several options for making a difference.
- Agree specific next steps.
- Check intention and outcomes have been met.
- Affirm relationship.

Follow-up
- Evaluate the interview.
- Record if appropriate.
- Pass on relevant and agreed information to other staff.
- Follow up with person counselled.

Suggested reading

Covey, Stephen, *The Seven Habits of Highly Effective People*. London: Simon & Schuster, 1992.
   A clear statement of what will enable leaders to be effective.

Dass, Ram, and Gorman, Paul, *How Can I Help?* New York: Alfred Knopf, Inc., 1985.
   A layman's guide to helping others with respect.

Dyer, Wayne, *You'll See It When You Believe It*. London: Arrow, 1990.
   A lovely and easy-to-read description of the power of our beliefs.

Heider, John, *The Tao of Leadership*. Aldershot: Wildwood House Ltd, 1986.
   A gentle way of recognizing the qualities and skills of a true leader.

Hoff, Benjamin, *The Tao of Pooh*. London: Mandarin, 1989.
   A delightful way to remind yourself of useful ways of being—one of my 'bibles'.

Hoff, Benjamin, *The Te of Piglet*. New York: Penguin, 1992.
   A useful follow-on to the first book, which looks at the different characteristics we have and their strengths and weaknesses.

Kamp, Di, *The Excellent Trainer*. London: Gower, 1996.
   In this book, I give a lot more information about how to take care of yourself as a trainer.

Kamp, Di, *The Dynamics of Excellence*. Worcester: Di Kamp, 1994.
   A set of audio tapes which take you through the techniques for developing your own potential, and that of others.

Laborde, Genie, *Influencing with Integrity*. Palo Alto, California: Syntony Publishing, 1987.
   An excellent book for developing your awareness of communication skills.

Peters, Tom, *Liberation Management*. London: Macmillan, 1992.
   Any of Tom Peters's work is good for challenging our old paradigms of how to be in the workplace.

Robbins, Anthony, *Unlimited Power*. London: Simon & Schuster, 1988.
  The simplest guide I know to empowerment of self and others.

Robbins, Anthony, *Awaken the Giant Within*. London: Simon & Schuster, 1992.
  A simple to follow guide to developing your inner abilities.

Rodgers, Carl, *Freedom to Learn for the 80's*. Columbus: Charles E. Merrill, 1983.
  This man gives an approach to professional counselling which is accessible to the layman, and well worth reading.

Semler, Ricardo, *Maverick*. London: Arrow, 1994.
  A wonderful description of a very different approach to running the workplace.

Senge, Peter, *The Fifth Discipline*. New York: Doubleday, 1994.
  A practical guide to the new skills required of managers.

Index